Praise for

What® to Expect When You're® Expected

...

"This story has it all—perfect pacing, organic character development, a plot that truly thickens, and a shock ending you literally won't see coming until the final spellbinding moments!" —*Publishers Trimesterly*

"I am in receipt of your check for $20. Here is the positive blurb you requested." —Stephen King

"Swim, don't wriggle, up your nearest Fallopian tube and land on a copy today!" —*The New York Pre*

"I'm as sure that this book is terrific as I am that, notwithstanding the provisions of sections 106 and 106A, the fair use of a copyrighted work for purposes such as criticism, comment, news reporting, teaching (including multiple copies for classroom use), scholarship, or research is not an infringement of copyright!" —The Copyright Act of 1976, § 107

"I wish you'd never been born! (Without reading this, that is!)" —Your father

ALSO BY DAVID JAVERBAUM

America (The Book): A Citizen's Guide to Democracy Inaction

WHAT® TO EXPECT
WHEN YOU'RE® EXPECTED

WHAT® TO EXPECT

WHEN YOU'RE® EXPECTED

A Fetus's Guide to the First Three Trimesters

David Javerbaum, G.E.D.

Illustrated by Mike Loew, O.G.

SPIEGEL & GRAU • NEW YORK • 2009

This book is a parody of *What to Expect When You're Expecting* by Heidi Murkoff, Arlene Eisenberg, and Sandee Hathaway B.S.N., published by Workman Publishing Company.

A Spiegel & Grau Trade Paperback Original

Copyight © 2009 by Bizzu LLC.

Published in the United States by Spiegel & Grau,
an imprint of The Random House Publishing Group,
a division of Random House, Inc., New York.

SPIEGEL & GRAU and Design is a registered trademark of Random House, Inc.

Photo credits are located on page 203.

LIBRARY OF CONGRESS CATALOGING-IN-PUBLICATION DATA
Javerbaum, David.
What to expect when you're expected: a fetus's guide to the
first three trimesters / David Javerbaum, G.E.D.
        p. cm.
Includes bibliographical references and index.
ISBN 978-0-385-52647-0
1. Pregnancy—Humor. 2. Fetus—Humor. I. Title.
PN6231.P68J38 2009
818'.5407—dc22   2009005970

PRINTED IN THE UNITED STATES OF AMERICA

www.spiegelandgrau.com

9 8 7 6 5 4 3 2 1

Book design by Casey Hampton

To the little child in some of us

FOREWORD
by The Stork

Irst of all, fuck you.

There was a time when I delivered every single baby in this country. Every . . . single . . . baby. If you were born between 1776 and the Kennedy assassination, you were one of mine.

And when you grew up and got curious about where you came from, Mom and Dad would set you straight: You came from me, the good ol' white stork, *Ciconia ciconia,* who carried you in a sling and dropped you down their chimney, or sometimes on the doorstep if they paid extra. This was how it was done. Do you understand this? *This was how it was done.*

Then, around '64 or '65, people started fuckin'.

At the time, I didn't think much of it. Seemed like another fad—Nehru jackets, civil rights, one of those things. But no. By the summer of '67 all these young kids, these sweet little cherubs I'd so carefully delivered to their grateful parents just twenty years before . . . all they were doing was fuckin'.

Now, I got no problem with people doing anything they want

in the privacy of their own homes. In fact, me and Mrs. Stork like to "ruffle feathers" now and then, if you know what I mean. Here is my problem: All this fuckin' somehow started leading to the procreation—through *sexual reproduction*—of actual human babies.

I know this is now considered "common practice." Let me assure you: It was not. It was most certainly *not* considered common practice for *Homo sapiens,* the world's most advanced species, to base its continued propagation on an activity that, all due respect, isn't fit to be performed in front of a squirrel.

My point is, there was a time when this book would have been unnecessary, because life was simple, and children were happy, and Santa Claus brought you presents and the Easter Bunny gave you candy and the Tooth Fairy paid good money for used molars and all was right with the world.

But apparently, the selfless generosity of Santa, Easter, Tooth, and me runs counter to the spirit of the Too Much Information Age, where God forbid a child should not know every excruciating detail about where babies come from or how they are fed or why they gush shit every hour like uncapped fire hydrants.

In other words, a book like this is now needed to help you get through the disillusionment caused by reading it.

As for me, I barely deliver babies anymore. A few in the South sometimes, the Bible Belt, but cities? Christ. I haven't flown business to New York since 1975.

—Thomas Harold Edward Stork

CONTENTS

Chapter 7

Month 5: Acknowledging Your Flailings................101

Chapter 8

Month 6: Threshold of Unabortability................117

Chapter 9

Month 7: Third Trime's the Charm................131

Chapter 10

Month 8: Allow Six to Eight Weeks for Delivery.............149

From the Author

I remember it like it was yesterday. Kate, my newborn, lay prone on our changing table, the very picture of infant curiosity and wonder. Suddenly, she turned to me with that wide-eyed expression so common to four-week-olds. "You know," she said, "somebody should write a guidebook for fetuses. Seriously. That's, like, a huge captive audience right there. Someone could probably make a ton of money off that. Hey, you gonna wipe or what?"

She was wise beyond her month. A trip to the bookstore found the "Parenting" racks full to bursting . . . but the empty shelves of the "Embryogenesizing" section told a far different story. There were literally no books—*not one*—written with the unborn reader in mind. At that moment I realized the time had come for a pregnancy guide aimed at a new generation. Specifically, the one being generated.

This, then, was the origin for *What® to Expect When You're® Expected,* which since its initial release in 2004 has sold an impressive 873 million copies. It's spawned a website, a series of

Japanese manga comics, and our new line of "Expected's Own" popcorn and salad dressing.

Naturally, I was thrilled by my work's success.* But I was even more excited by the letters and e-mails I received from thousands of pre- and newborns. Many expressed gratitude not merely for the book, but for the discovery that they were not alone, that other human beings were also going through the same strange, at times bewildering process of being born.

There were also a few marriage proposals. These were disturbing.

Many respondents voiced concerns and quibbles about some of the book's contents. This new edition reflects this feedback. Hence, the "Cocktails for Babies" section has been omitted, and greater focus has been placed on health and diet, with fewer pages devoted to automotive repair.

While these changes make for a more accurate text, this book should still not be seen as "comprehensive," even if it is much, much heavier than you. The truth is, no guide can anticipate every problem or calibrate every circumstance of your particular fetalcy. It is as unique as the particular combination of neuroses, angst, and naïveté that are your parents.

I end with a thank-you to my darling daughter, whose simple idea inspired a phenomenon . . . and a failed lawsuit. Sorry, Kate, but you heard what the nice judge said: Children under ten can't file for copyright.

—*David Javerbaum, G.E.D.*

---

* I was less thrilled with the movie adaptation. Vin Diesel was *not* my first choice for "Fetus."

WHAT® TO EXPECT WHEN YOU'RE® EXPECTED

CHAPTER 1

Conception
When Wanted Life Begins

So you're a zygote. Congratulations! Existence is one of the most exciting things that will ever happen to you.

You are the end result of both four billion years of evolution and three minutes of rubbing. In the cosmic sense, the question of where we come from, along with that of where we go when—spoiler alert!—we die, are the unfathomable conundrums bookending our brief time on earth. But such metaphysical niceties are, perhaps, too abstract for a lay zygote like yourself. So let's focus on the more immediate causes.

"THE TALK"

"Where do babies come from? And when will I get to be one?"

We'll begin with **your mother**. Word is she's so dumb, she hears it's chilly outside and gets a bowl. More to the point, she's also fertile, and last month, she released an **ovum**, or egg, from its dank cell inside the women's prison known as her **ovary**. No

Fig.1. *On Sunday mornings, many sperm enjoy ova Benedict.*

doubt this ovum expected to end up like most or all its older siblings—as part of a small red spot on the white pants Mom foolishly wore to the company picnic. But a different fate was in store
for it, a rendezvous with a milky sausagefest known as **semen**.
This liquid comes from **your father**, and given his track record,
the hundreds of millions of **sperm** comprising it no doubt *also*
expected a grisly end (see chart, p. 5). But last night, inspired by
pornography and/or the faded memory of a high-school girlfriend, your father inserted his erect penis, or "**pee-pee**," into
your mother's vagina, or "**cooch**." They then engaged in a once
filthy act now rendered dispiritingly functional. When the semen
wrangling was over, five hundred million microscopic demi-Q-
tips were discharged intra-coochally. What followed was a brutal
ordeal, with contestants forced to swim the equivalent of hundreds of miles upstream with no map and no compass . . . all
while *literally* flagellating themselves. It was exactly like *Fear
Factor,* only it wasn't hosted by Joe Rogan. So at least it was better than *Fear Factor.*

YOUR FATHER'S SPERM: WHERE ARE THEY NOW?

LOCATION	NUMBER OF SPERM
Sheet	200,000,000,000 (est.)
Pillowcase	150,000,000,000 (est.)
Kleenex	145,000,000,000 (est.)
Shower	85,000,000,000 (est.)
Ceiling fan	55,000,000,000 (est.)
Bearskin rug	33,000,000,000 (est.)
Wrestling mat (1991 county championships)	33,000,000,000 (est.)
Women	21,000,000,000 (est.)
Men	2,100,000,000 (est.)
Women's athletic-wear department of Modell's Sporting Goods	500,000,000 (est.)
Room 231, Comfort Inn, Elkhart, Ind.	500,000,000 (est.)
Biscuit in frat-house basement	500,000,000 (est.)
You	1 (exactly)

Chart courtesy Guccione Institute for Masturbation Studies

The carnage left your mother's birth canal looking like a Civil War battlefield, and as with those battlefields, the scene had probably been reenacted many times before. But this time was different. This time, one sperm managed to overcome the odds and arrive at his destiny—fair Lady Ovum. Their conversation was the stuff of legend.

SPERM: 'Tsup.

EGG: 'Tsup.

   [*Awkward pause*]

SPERM: So, I guess we should, ummm . . .

EGG: Yeah.

   [SPERM *begins penetration.*]

SPERM: Does this feel good?

EGG: Does *what* feel good?

SPERM: Yikes.

The sperm passed through the ovum's outer protective layers—the **corona radiata**, the **zona pellucida**, and the **moat**

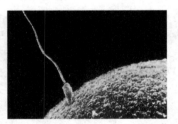

Fig. 2. *In eighteen years, this will need $300,000 for college.*

—until finally reaching its creamy nougat center, where, after one last bumping of uglies, **you** were created (Fig. 2).

Disappointed? Perhaps you'd hoped your entrée into life would be more "cherubs playing trumpet fanfares" and less "heaping dollops of human ejaculate." This is a common preconception, pre-conception. But in truth, yours *was* a noble genesis. It turns out nature has a goo fetish. Life itself started with primeval soup.* Ever since, the rule has been: The more complex the species, the ickier its creation. Well, you are earth's highest life-form, and by

---

* It then had the primeval salad.

You're Welcome!

You'll notice that this book makes many references to traditional family relationships, using terms like "housewives," "polygamy," and *"patriarchal hegemony."* By no means is this meant to exclude those fetuses and newborns whose families are more "untraditional"— those in which the mother aspires to a career, for example, or for whom the priest's Nuptial Blessing during the Sacrament of Matrimony was in English rather than Latin. These terms are simply a way of avoiding more cumbersome phrases, like "distorted families," "violators of divine providence," and "San Franciscans." Our hope is that you will mentally take note of any phrase in this book that doesn't fit your lifestyle, then simply modify your lifestyle to fit that phrase.

the time you're born, you'll be covered in so much gunk you'll look like Gollum in chowder!

A final note: There is a very tiny chance your origin involved neither sperm nor egg, but rather **the Word of God breathing flesh into the womb of a Blessed Virgin**. If this is the case, man, have we been waiting for You!

WOMB WITH A VIEW

"I'm in a petri dish, and a lot of what you've said so far doesn't make sense."

That's because you're a **test-tube baby**, and an abomination against the will of God. Unlike regular, or "normal," children, you were created when a doctor removed ova kicking and screaming from their natural habitat and marinated them in sperm that are, in all likelihood, his. (Shhhhhhh!) You'll be waiting in a lab for three to five days, so use this time to soak in the glories of the outside world—the Medi-Sharps collection bin, the overhead fluorescent light, the lab technician.* Eventually, an embryologist will judge you based on evenness of growth, degree of fragmentation, and talent. (Tip: Don't sing "Stayin' Alive." It comes off desperate.) If all goes well, it's just a hop, skip, and a catheter ride back inside Mommy. If not, welcome to the exciting stem-cell research debate!

WERE YOU AN OOPSIE?

"I heard that if the tail on the sperm that conceived me bent to the left it means I was an accident. Is this true or just an old eggs' tale?"

UTERINE LINER NOTE

"I always suspected I was a 'love child,' but I didn't know for sure until I was eight and my mother got drunk and told me I was an accident, I'd ruined her life, and she wished I was never born. Whew! Finally, closure!"

—Charles Manson, San Quentin State Prison

It is natural to wonder if you were the deliberate creation of two people in love, or the unintended by-product of an office party at Outback Steakhouse gone horribly awry. Alas, none of the widely circulated "methods" of determining intent have any scientific validity, be they the bend of the sperm's tail, the thickness of the zona pellucida, or the notorious infantile taunt,

If you see the epiblast,
Mommy has a child at last.
If the hypoblast is first,
Daddy's rubber musta burst!

Nevertheless, in this enlightened age of birth control, single motherhood, and enough Internet porn for mankind to shoot off a

---

* Her name is Dawn, she is very lonely, and the sight of you only adds to her heartache.

cum rope to Neptune every six minutes, it is doubtful you were a total accident. Indeed, it's far more likely you were the extremely *un*accidental result of either the test-tube procedure or some other method, such as **hormone injections**, **ovarian stimulation**, **artificial insemination**, **frozen-embryo transfers**, **vaginatherapy**, **cervical spelunking**, **testicular taunting**, **turkey basterectomy**, **Wiccan acupuncture**, **gingerroot douches**, **oyster enemas**, **sperm bidets**, **Sybian colonics**, **intrauterine feng shui**, **epatoscomancy** (divination of the entrails of sacrificed animals), and/or **stealing a baby from a hospital**.

Besides, even if your parents *didn't* mean for you to happen, that has no bearing whatsoever on your intrinsic worth as a human being. It just greatly reduces the chances that you'll get to *be* one.

CODE DEPENDENCY

"Help! My parents just gave me this 'DNA' stuff, and now it's telling me exactly what to do. Why are they bossing me around?! I'm my own cell!"

DNA—which stands for "Do Not Alter," the directive it stamps on your soul—is a substance so incredibly potent, it can be used to frame you for murder at the age of eight cells. Chemically, of course, it's a polymerous series of double-helical nucleotides with an ester-bonded sugar/phosphate backbone linking four purine or pyrimidine bases: Awesome Apple®, Chillin' Cherry®, Groovylicious Grape®, and Thrillin' Thymine®. When a sperm fertilizes an egg, their DNA merge into units called **genes**. They're an even split, belonging half to your mother and half to your father, just as *you* will after their prolonged custody battle a few years down the road. These genes are organized into larger units called **chromosomes**, and this is probably a good

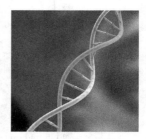

Fig. 3. *Godzilla's DNA (actual size).*

Determinism at Work: A Sample Genome

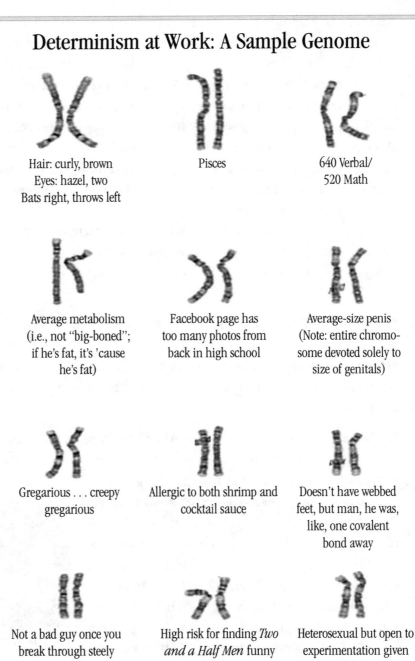

Hair: curly, brown
Eyes: hazel, two
Bats right, throws left

Pisces

640 Verbal/
520 Math

Average metabolism
(i.e., not "big-boned";
if he's fat, it's 'cause
he's fat)

Facebook page has
too many photos from
back in high school

Average-size penis
(Note: entire chromo-
some devoted solely to
size of genitals)

Gregarious . . . creepy
gregarious

Allergic to both shrimp and
cocktail sauce

Doesn't have webbed
feet, but man, he was,
like, one covalent
bond away

Not a bad guy once you
break through steely
veneer

High risk for finding *Two
and a Half Men* funny

Heterosexual but open to
experimentation given
right person
and atmosphere of trust

Excellent problem-causing
skills

Unscrews Oreos
before eating

Always with the
knock-knock jokes

Carries recessive
gene for messy room—
will pass on to children

Couldn't get AIDS
if he bottomed all
of Chelsea

~~Direct descendent of Jesus
and Mary Magdalene~~

Squanders every
goddamn opportunity he
ever gets

Immortal. Kidding!
Dies of heart failure
at age seventy-eight

Favorite tennis
surface: clay

Able to do this one trick with his elbows that used to be kind of
cool but now just seems stupid, but not even stupid enough to
get on *Letterman,* but he still does it at parties when he's had
enough to drink and thinks it's entertaining but everybody's
seen it before and it's just embarrassing

Fan of '80s punk
band X

Married to Gloria
Sterling of Providence,
Rhode Island

*Chromosome sample courtesy cigarette butt retrieved from garbage can outside home of
Richard Sterling, Providence, Rhode Island*

time for you to do a self-inventory of those, because you're going to want to have forty-six. Like, *exactly*. If you're missing a couple, stop what you're doing and find them.* Anyhoo, these chromosomes form your instruction manual, and the new science of genome analysis is now revealing some of the mysteries contained within (see chart, p. 10).

But though your genes are something over which you have no control, take heart: Your development will be just as profoundly shaped by your upbringing, over which you have merely *almost* no control. Though the perennial "Nature versus Nurture" debate was resolved 5–4 for Nature by the Supreme Court in 2003, it's now clear the two forces actually work in conjunction. *Nature* may preordain that you're a serial killer, but it is *nurture* that will determine your preferred victim type and method of death. Similarly, the *nurture* of a warm, loving family will in the end serve only to highlight your true *nature* as a parasitic slacker living in their basement. So to address your initial complaint: Don't waste your time in the womb resenting your parents. You have your whole life ahead of you for that.†

A Fetal Examination®
PARENTAL DIAGNOSIS: ALLAYING YOUR FEARS

Eyes, hair color, personality: Fetalcy is a time of uncertainty when it comes to many subjects. Most of these prompt little more than fun debate. But there's one question no embryo likes to joke about, one few even want to discuss: "Are my parents idiots?"

---

* If you're missing twelve, you might want to refer to our other book, *What to Expect When You're a Porcupine.*
† Note: A handful of scientists believe true self-actualization emerges from neither nature *nor* nurture but a long process of introspection, sacrifice, and authentic life experience. They are stupid and no fun.

Until recently, that question could only be answered at birth. But breakthroughs in the field of **parental diagnosis** mean it's now possible to find out as early as the middle of the first trimester whether your mommy and daddy have any idea what they're doing. Most embryos and fetuses choose not to avail themselves of this option, preferring to cling as long as possible to the faint hope their parents aren't a few bricks shy of a load. But for those in high-risk categories, the benefits of parental diagnosis outweigh the risks. Good candidates include those unborns whose mom or dad

- is over thirty-five and still has a ponytail
- has been exposed, since your conception, to over ten minutes of *The Real Housewives of New York City*
- is already resented by previous children
- consider themselves well prepared for parenting because "they have two nieces they're soooo close with"
- has an infant-sized Che Guevara T-shirt all picked out for you
- is a Cubs fan

TYPES OF TESTS

There are now dozens of tests used to help determine if your parents are neither all that nor a bag of chips. These include analyses of TV habits, iPod playlists, ball-scratching frequency, even voting records.* Among the best known are the following:

QUAD SCREENING

What is it? In quad screening, a technician draws a sample of your parents' blood and tests it for the presence of four sub-

---

* Nader '04 = mandatory adoption.

stances: Schlitz, patchouli, Chef Boyardee's Dinosaurs with Mini Meatballs, and horse tranquilizer.

What does it prove? The presence of one of these increases the risk that your parents are incompetent. The presence of all of them indicates that you are the Antichrist.

VIGOROUS CHRONIC SAMPLING (VCS)

What is it? In the presence of a specially trained obstetrician, Mommy and Daddy toke a fat blunt of da chronic, carefully removed from Snoop Dogg's crib.

What does it prove? If a stranger in a lab coat was able to convince them to smoke some of Snoop Dogg's shit, homeys got shit-ass judgment.

ULTRASUEDE® TESTING

What is it? Parents are given swatches of Ultrasuede®—a remarkable space-age microfiber that feels exactly like suede but is stain- and discoloration-resistant—and asked to rub them with dirt, wine, and tomato sauce. They then clean the stains off with simple soap and water.

What does it prove? The remarkable durability of Ultrasuede®!

FABIOCENTESIS

What is it? In a very invasive procedure, a team of child-welfare agents raid your mother's bookshelves looking for novels with Fabio on the cover.

What does it prove? She has too much free time.

WORST-CASE SCENARIO

Parental diagnoses quite frequently reveal that Mommy and Daddy are suffering from severe **uncertainty**, **insecurity**, and **purposeless gnawing dread**. This is a good sign. It shows that they've begun developing the contemporary parenting skills they'll need to replace the **love**, **innate common sense**, and **three-million-year-old stockpile of genetic wisdom** they might otherwise have foolishly relied on. But what if the tests reveal more? What if there *is* patchouli? What if da chronic *does* blow their mizz-inds? What if dozens of volumes in Mommy's bookcase *are* adorned by Fabio's shirtless majesty?

It's an intensely personal decision. While terminating your parents is a constitutionally protected right (at least for now), it is still a harrowing and frankly somewhat self-destructive proposition. The truth is only .03 percent of parents are absolutely perfect. The remaining 99.97 percent can pretty much be counted on to act like total dumbasses at some or all parts of your life.

So yes, in all likelihood there is indeed something profoundly wrong with your parents. But is it worth doing something drastic about? Probably not. First off, most kids take great pleasure in discovering how ill equipped Mom and Dad truly are. You may even come to grow fond of them as they cutely flail about, acting like they have the slightest clue about how to raise you. More important, they're not alone. As parenting skills have declined over the last few decades, America has responded with **parenting experts, childbirth counselors, lactation consultants, couvade mentors, contraction managers, doulas, midwives, hypnobirthers, prenatal uterine masseuses, Ayurvedic newborn karmographers, baby whisperers, baby yellers, baby sign-language teachers, baby yoga, baby Pilates, baby pole dancing, babyproof toilet locks/door stoppers/drawer catches/outlet plugs/corner cushions/crib tents/nonslip heat-sensitive color-changing bath appliqués/twenty-four-hour infrared** video monitors with wet-diaper cowbell alarms/twenty-gallon jars of Purell, nipple shields, hooter hiders, flexishield areola stimulators, wind-powered breast pumps, at-home sonograms, wiper warmers, wiper warmer cozies, pregnancy books, pregnancy journals, pregnancy nutrition journals, gay pregnancy nutrition journals, "baby bumps," expectant celebrities whose fetuses outweigh them, *American Baby*, *Fit Pregnancy*, *Parenting*, *MILF Parenting*, other maternity magazines no one actually subscribes to but that make people feel guilty when they see them in pediatric waiting rooms, message boards, chat rooms, fear blogs, scare spam, scientific studies, unscientific studies, alarming anecdotes about friends of friends, news items about sixty-five-year-old Italian women carrying their granddaughters' quints, and thousands of other components making up what President Eisenhower called "**the maternity-industrial complex.**"

So buck up! You won't be battling your parents' craziness alone. You'll have the *world's* craziness right alongside you.

CHAPTER 2

Throughout Your Fetalcy

Unborn babies have always worried. (Hence, their "fetal position.") *What* they worry about, however, has changed considerably over the generations. Hundreds of years ago, your forefetuses worried that a slap on Mommy's belly might leave them with a hand-shaped birthmark, or that her penchant for bananas would turn them into gorillas. The march of science proved these fears wrong and treatable, respectively.

Today's fetus has its own array of concerns. It seems every activity your mother engages in raises questions: *Should* she be shooting heroin? Is crop dusting *really* a good idea? How much rugby is *too* much rugby? And *when* can I get more of that delicious heroin? Calm down. As discussed in the last chapter, you're not alone in your battle for survival against the woman giving you life. A vast army is working to imbue Mommy with the baseline alarmism she needs to ensure you emerge safe and healthy from her **hoo-ha** in forty weeks.

What You May Be Concerned She's Not Concerned About

PRACTITIONER, PRACTITIONER, PRACTITIONER

"I really think my mother needs professional help."

And she's going to get it! The days of going through pregnancy and labor with little or no medical supervision are over.* Today's

gravida has access to a wide variety of professionals armed with the knowledge, equipment, and vague anecdotal evidence to remove any stress *you* may be feeling and put it squarely where it belongs—in Mommy's brain.

The first decision Mommy must make (and Daddy must obediently acquiesce to) is what type of practitioner is right for her. Most women select an **obstetrician** for their care. Despite their snobby reputations for having "degrees from medical school" and "years of rigorous training," obstetricians can actually be quite personable and reassuring; the most skilled pepper their conversations with phrases like "heck," "shucks," and "now, don't this vag-

Fig. 4. *Early obstetrical practice was hampered by societal prudery. Above, a Victorian woman gives birth as a midwife huddles beneath her hoop skirt.*

inal discharge just beat all?" Ten to twelve percent of women choose a **family practitioner** (**FP**). FPs are the decathletes of medicine—pretty good at lots of stuff, but not great at anything in particular. They're a good choice for a woman looking for a doctor to not only help her have a healthy baby but cure her sore throat, set her broken wrist, and write her "friendly" prescriptions

* Except for two billion people.

for Percocet. A third option is a **midwife**. Midwives are trained to see Mommy as a person rather than a patient and are more willing to take the time to talk with her about her emotional wellbeing. They are total wastes of money.

A related question concerns the **type of practice** Mommy will choose. She may develop a strong bond with a **solo practitioner**, but if he or she is in Tahiti come labor, you might end up extracted by Dr. Random B. Strangerfingers. This will not be the case with a **group practice**, but she may receive conflicting advice from different doctors, and as they say, "A man with one watch knows what time it is; a man with two is never sure."* Then there are the midwife-run **birthing centers** that first emerged in the 1970s. These are widely distrusted, as they first emerged in the 1970s.

Whichever type of caregiver and practice your mother chooses, she owes it to her health insurance plan, and to a lesser extent you, to make the most of their relationship by doing the following:

- *Taking thorough notes at each scheduled appointment.* That means coming prepared with a pen, index cards, a looseleaf notebook, safety scissors, a six-pack of glue sticks, and a Speed Racer Activity Binder.
- *Telling the truth.* The doctor needs to obtain a complete picture of Mommy's pregnancy, so she must be forthright when asked about her drug use, her obstetrical history, the state of her marriage, her level of sexual fulfillment, whether she finds the doctor attractive, and what she is doing this Friday.
- *Keeping up-to-date.* If Mommy reads something new or just interesting about pregnancy in the paper or a magazine or

---

* And a gynecologist with one watch who *had* two before Mommy's appointment . . . well, he's in all kinds of trouble.

on a website, she should make multiple printouts, race to her doctor's office, interrupt him in the middle of whatever he's doing, and inform him of this new thing about which he would not otherwise have heard because it's not like he's a doctor who keeps up with this stuff.

- *Exercising judgment.* As mentioned earlier, it is not uncommon in a group practice for two doctors to give the same patient slightly different advice. When this happens, it is because one of them is deliberately trying to screw with Mommy's head. She should lock them in a room together and make them argue until one of them admits they were just fucking around to win a bet.
- *Never hesitating to call.* If questions arise between scheduled visits, Mommy shouldn't be afraid her concerns will sound silly or ridiculous. Phoning the doctor will not only ease her mind, it will provide the doctor's entire staff with untold amusement as they gather around the phone rolling their eyes and stifling laughter at her comically baseless anxiety.

If all goes well, Mommy and the doctor will hit it off swimmingly, and not only will you be in capable hands, but that nose job she's always wanted will wind up submitted to Blue Cross as a "pregnancy-related rhinoplasty"!

FEMME FETALE

"My mother just took a sip of white wine. Am I going to end up looking like some Chernobyl baby now?"

An ounce of white wine won't hurt you, especially a dry, light-bodied one (Fig. 5). In fact, you'd probably emerge unscathed from *two* ounces of a good Muscadet. But in general, drinking

Fig. 5. *"With a peach aroma and a delightfully chalky mouth-feel, a small glass of Chéreau-Cartré Château de Chesnaie Muscadet is totally worth the risk for pregnant women."*
—*Robert Parker,* Wine Spectator

while expecting is like drinking and driving: It takes a lot of practice to do it right. So unless your mother's mastered the art by imbibing non-stop for her last three pregnancies, it's best for you that she abstain from alcohol entirely.

Why? For starters, you're a minor. You cannot legally consume alcohol for twenty-one years and will not *actually* do so for at least eleven. Giving you booze could lead to criminal prosecution of your mom, which would be a real shame, since she's clearly pretty cool, what with her giving you booze and all. More to the point, alcohol has devastating effects on your growing body. Overwhelming scientific evidence suggests that the children of mothers who drink are born incoherent, near-sighted, and incontinent. They tend to show poor judgment and will be drawn to any nipple they see, a phenomenon known as "beer ga-ga-ing." Particularly at risk are so-called **Jack Daniels kids**, who are born with abnormally high levels of both lynyrdism and skynyrdism.

Alas, teetotaling itself may pose a risk for your mother. In women accustomed to social drinking, the sudden imposed abstinence can induce **maternal non-alcohol syndrome** (**MNAS**), a condition characterized by irritability, depression, and a sudden nostalgia for the days of sorority parties and two-for-one Sex on the Beach Nights at Ruby Tuesday, a halcyon era of youth and irresponsibility gone forever now, never to return, never ever.* But most moms learn to overcome MNAS with a strict regimen of guilt, fruit juice, and dirty looks from other people at the bar.

A final note: Pregnant mommies often ask their husbands to refrain from drinking alcohol in solidarity. Daddies often protest

* Ever.

> ### UTERINE LINER NOTE
>
> *"Mommy quit smoking in my second trimester, but by that point I was addicted and in no position to make a cigarette run. I had to go cold turkey. It was a tough few weeks—I was fidgety and I gained a lot of weight—but I kicked the habit by my birth. But sometimes I still find myself fighting the urge to light my thumb."*
>
> —Madison B., three months old,
> Columbus, Ohio

on the grounds that *their* drinking has no effect on *your* health. In most cases, the marriage is fundamentally sound and a compromise is reached: Daddy agrees not to get caught.

YOUR MOM'S SMOKIN'

"Mommy smokes a pack of menthols a day. Is that why I feel so emphysemic and minty fresh?"

'Fraid so. The old expression is true: Gestating in a smoker really *is* like inseminating an ashtray. Compared with nonsmokers', smokers' fetuses are much smaller and lighter, and look only slightly cooler. In addition, the smoke-filled environment gives the entire uterus a film noir vibe many fetuses find pretentious. These babies emerge from their live-in wombidor more susceptible to nearly every childhood disease, even cooties.

Dude! Question for Ya!

"I think my mom smokes pot. [Long pause] My placenta is so spirally!"

Illicit **marijuana** use increases the chances of unborn children suffering prolonged labor, tremors, and vision abnormalities. *Medical* marijuana, however, is harmless, because that's legal. Put another way, if Mom's toking heavy-duty

Fig. 6. *The Star Child from* 2001: A Space Odyssey *was so high he came in his own dime bag.*

Kali Mist, you've got an appointment with Schwaggy von Freakout, but if she be kiefing da Man's golden leaf ja Rasta self can go on gazin' atcha navel, mon. Which is it? Let's go with the best-case scenario and assume your mother has glaucoma.

Hard Drugs, Slightly Less Hard Choices

"From an obstetrical viewpoint, crack cocaine . . . Good? Bad? Little of both?"

Mainly bad. In fact, this is a good time for Mommy to seriously consider eliminating (or at least curtailing) her daily crack use. The same applies to opiates such as heroin and morphine. Hallucinogens like LSD are even more dangerous; the same chemicals that give adults a mind-blowing trip back to the womb would send you on a soul-crushing trip *forward* in time, to the bleak office cubicle where you will one day work as an assistant account manager.

Trust Us!

This book has already made several references to "recent studies." For purposes of concision, we will follow the example of contemporary media outlets and fail to mention who did the studying, what and how many people were studied, who published the study, which corporations with vested interests in the results helped pay for it, and whether or not the whole thing isn't just based on some story one of the publisher's interns "thinks she heard this one time." *Just trust us.* They are recent studies, they are completely authoritative, and when they "suggest" something, take it in the same spirit as Stalin "suggesting" you stop by the Kremlin for a little chat.

WHAT ABOUT CRYSTAL METH?

"What about crystal meth?"

Nah, that's fine.

VENTI ICED NO-WHIP DOPPIO SOY BABYCCINO

"Should Mom give up coffee for me?"

This is a matter of some controversy. On the one hand, numerous studies have shown absolutely no link between caffeine and pregnancy problems. On the other hand . . . you'd just *think* there would be, right? It's so weird.

For now, the consensus is that you're in no danger from Mommy's **coffee** drinking, provided it's in moderation (that is, under forty cups a day). Frankly, this is one indulgence you might want to cut Mommy some slack on. She's already giving up booze, weed, and horse tranquilizers for you, and it's a lot to ask her to get through the next nine months without any chemical enhancement whatsoever. Yes, the caffeine may keep you up all night, but what, like you've got work tomorrow?

One thing Mommy *does* need to give up, however, is **herbal tea**, which science has proven, time and time again, turns boys lesbian.

APOCALYPSE MEOW

"I'm concerned because Mommy has two cats, and I've heard they can carry a disease that could harm me. Also, I'm more of a dog embryo."

First off, it's rather amazing that you even exist, since women with multiple cats are generally **unattractive** and **lonely**. Anyway, the disease you're referring to is **toxoplasmosis**, and it's transmitted primarily through the ingestion of cat feces (along with unpasteurized milk). So you should be in no danger assuming your mother follows the six basic rules of toxoplasmosis prevention:

Fig. 7. *This is one household nuisance you may find un-"bear"-able!*

- Don't eat cat shit.
- Don't eat food on which a cat has shit.
- Don't eat litter boxes.
- After sticking your finger in your cat's anus, use Purell.
- At restaurants, never order your meat *à la merde du chat*.
- If you *must* eat cat shit, pasteurize it.

SAUNAGRAM

Fig. 8. *At age fifty, Antonio Banderas is still* muy *caliente!*

"What about our hot tub? Mommy likes to use it every Wednesday with Secret Daddy."

Anything that can raise Mommy's body temperature beyond 102 degrees Fahrenheit (46.5 kilometers) is potentially hazardous to your health. This means your mother should be wary of prolonged exposure not only to **hot tubs** but **saunas**, **electric blankets**, **pizza ovens**, **the center of the sun**, and **Antonio Banderas** (Fig. 8).

On the plus side, the worries concerning **microwave ovens** are totally unfounded. Microwaves are *completely* safe for use by *any* pregnant woman wearing the standard hazmat suit, lead apron, and industrial goggles, and most incidents of accidental exposure can be remedied with a simple **decontamination shower** (Fig. 9).

Fig. 9. *A nuclear technician decontaminates a pregnant woman who ventured too close to a simmering Hot Pocket.*

CAN YOU HEAR ME NOW?

"Mom talks on her cell phone all day. Like, three feet from my head. It's . . . it's just so fucking rude."

It is, but alas, there is no scientific evidence that cell phone babies face any *physical* risk. Psychologically, of course, it's another story. Mommy's constant yammering not only feels rude, it makes it hard for you to concentrate, sleep, or get anything done. Be patient, little embryo. In nine short months, revenge will be thine.

Ask an Old Wife

Old wives are bottomless wells of wisdom. Throughout this book, we will be turning to Hortence Gwinnett, one of America's oldest and wiviest people, for common-sense answers to some of your trickiest questions.

Q: Is it okay if Mommy takes a bath?

A: O sweet merciful heavens no! If she puts so much as one toe in that tub, the water-germs will shoot up her woman-parts faster than you can say "consumption"! My cousin Petunia immersed herself but one time her whole fecundity, and her poor baby Hyacinth was born without skin! If your mother insists on abluting herself, she must do so only with a vellum sponge daubed lightly in talcum, and she must rinse within the hour in an emulsion of ambergris and bee's milk!

Thanks for thy question!

SLAUGHTERHOUSE OR SLAUGHTERHOME?

"What household hazards should I be worried that Mommy isn't worrying about?"

Funny you should ask:

Lead. Recent studies suggest that fetuses do best when their mothers avoid foods rich in lead, such as pencils and Victorian-era sewer pipes.

Household cleaning products. Your mother should learn the mnemonic device, "My cookies look wicked cool!" It's an easy way to remember that Mr. Clean, Lysol, Windex, and Clorox are the *only* four household cleaning products safe to drink.

Tap water. Completely safe, so long as you pass it through a basic filter, give it a made-up name like Dasani, and charge schmucks three dollars a bottle for it.

Whatever it is making those creepy howling noises every full moon. Should be investigated ASAP, preferably by descending into the basement with one of those old-timey lanterns (Fig. 10).

Insecticides. Worse than having no contaminants in you, but better than having insects in you.

Fig. 10. *It beckons.*

Paint fumes. There was a time when all paints were either lead-based, mercury-enhanced, or plutonium-flavored. That's no longer the case, but for safety's sake it's still best to let Dad take charge of painting your room and let Mommy handle related matters, like choosing the color and then later saying it doesn't look as vibrant on the wall as she pictured it based on the sample and maybe they should have gone with the foam green.

A Fetal Examination®
NUTRITION: YOU ARE WHAT SHE EATS

"So," you may be asking yourself, "how's the food in this place?" Answer: Eh. Truth is, you won't be tasting much of anything,

Fig. 11. *Having vanquished all three meals, the burrito takes a well-earned nap.*

even after you grow a tongue, because you will be receiving all your nutriments through the **umbilical cord**,* a gelatinous lasso originally conceived as a belly-button cozy. It's a nice little tube, and you'll soon grow attached to it.

Ordering all your meals in *is* convenient. But it's also risky. You're putting your diet in Mommy's hands, and **good nutrition** is not something Americans are known for. The old cliché that pregnant women are "eating for two" is true only insofar as *every* American eats for two. At least two. Five, in Alabama. Many expectant American moms have even come to believe that eating healthy may *endanger* their unborn child. They fear it will set him up as an outcast in a society that, at some point in the nineties, deemed the burrito a worthy addition to the breakfast table (Fig. 11).

Of course, you'll have as little control over *what* Mommy puts in her body as you did over *who*. But here are a few dietary principles she'll (hopefully!) be practicing:

Count calories—but not too many. The average pregnant woman needs only three hundred *additional* calories a day. Nice to know the daily energy needed to kickstart life can be satisfied by a Snickers bar, or by simply *staring at the wrapper* of a Triple Whopper® with cheese.

* Also known as "the navel attaché."

UTERINE LINER NOTE

"I like to kick my cord blood up a notch—throw in a little garlic, Tabasco, cayenne pepper . . . toss in a few crawfish. Bam! Now that's gumbo!"

—Tiffany Lagasse, Week 28, New Orleans, Louisiana

If Mommy Loves You . . .

. . . she'll replace her favorite snack foods with these low-fat alternatives.

Instead of . . .	*She'll have . . .*
Potato chips	Soy Crisps
Pretzels	Soybeans
Soy sauce	Soy soy
Oysters	Soysters
Donuts	Don'tnuts
Chicken (fried)	Chicken (powdered)
Pint of ice cream	28 quarts of frozen yogurt
Birthday cake	Veterans' Day Triscuit
Chocolate brioche	*Chocolat* with Juliette Binoche
French fries	French lessons
Flavor	Sadness

Redefine "meals." Instead of the usual three, some mommies find it easier to have six meals a day, each one half-sized. Conversely, others prefer having one meal during the entire pregnancy, 810 times larger than a typical one.

Ride out the cravings. Most pregnant women experience sudden cravings for some foods—generally, delicious ones—and sudden aversions to others—many of which, oddly enough, taste bad. It's not clear why this happens. Some blame hormones, others vestigial instincts; those of a darker turn see the whole thing as a sinister mind-control experiment underwritten by the Vlasic pickle company (Fig. 12). There are healthy alternatives to many of the most common snack foods (see chart on page 30), but Mommy's best bet for riding out the cravings may be **sublimating**, a strategy Daddy can help her with (see recipe on next page).

Fig. 12. *The Vlasic spokesbird works with the Mafia to implant biochemical nerve chips in the frontal lobes of pregnant women.*

The fresher, the better. Fresh fruit is the healthiest; raw vegetables have the most vitamins; beef has more protein when gnawed off a living cow; and maple syrup should be sucked out of the tree (Fig. 13).

ig. 13. *A "Montpelier marriage."*

Water, water everywhere. Like the earth, Mommy's body is mostly water, and like the earth, the ratio is increasing ominously all the time. Mommy should have at least eight cups a day of liquid, fluid, drinkable, nonviscous watery beverages. This will not only keep you healthy but also reduce Mommy's risk of swelling, urinary tract infection, and sitting through a movie.

The Pill, Part Two. Many mommies take **prenatal supplements**. These basketball-sized, volleyball-flavored vitamin tablets are loaded with important minerals like folic acid, rubies, and calcium. While helpful "backups," these are *not* to be viewed as replacements for a good diet. Rather, they are replacements for a bad one.

I Scream, You Scream

1 groggy Daddy

1 hormonal Mommy

1 oven-enclosed bun

3 A.M.

4 simple goddamn requests for a scoop of Ben & Jerry's Chunky
   Monkey

1 derisive comment re Mommy's weight gain, coarsely spoken

50–100 long-standing suppressed issues putting the very foundation of
   the marriage in question

$\frac{1}{2}$- hearted apology

Place bun in oven; set timer for 8 months. Arrange Daddy and Mommy
on sheet. Add first simple goddamn request. Continue adding simple
goddamn requests with greater frequency until tempers flare and moods
harden. Insert derisive comment. Let suppressed issues putting very
foundation of marriage in question rise. Finish with ½-hearted apology.
Allow Daddy to cool on couch.

Note: For a sweeter result, finish with a dollop of Ben & Jerry's Chunky
Monkey.

SERVES NO PURPOSE.

Avoid listeria. Listeria is a bacteria that can cause listeriosis, lis-
teritis, Lister's disease, and, in extreme cases, prolonged listering.
To avoid it and similar ailments, it's best that Mommy stay away
from the following foods:

Fig. 14. *The thermometerfish fools predators into thinking it's undercooked.*

- **Deli meat.** Can be highly contaminated; should only be consumed after a thorough chemical bath in such antibacterial agents as lettuce, tomato, and mustard.
- **Fish with mercury.** To be especially avoided: The North Atlantic thermometerfish (Fig. 14).
- **Smoked seafood.** Lox, nova, and whitefish? Remember them in your next Kaddish.
- **Unpasteurized milk.**
- **Unsimonized dry cleaning.**
- **Soft cheese.** But hard cheese is fine. How soft is too soft? Here's a rule of thumb: Throw the cheese against the wall, then lick the wall. If the wall tastes like cheese . . . too soft.

Eat food. Seems obvious, but some pregnant women suffer from **pica**, a disorder characterized by an appetite for nonfoods such as dirt, clay, or paper. This may be why you've noticed small bits of pottery and/or *Vanity Fair* in your placenta. Don't panic; Mommy will work it out. In the meantime, sit back, relax, and take in the glamorously literate *Weltanschauung* of Graydon Carter.

Get Daddy's help. Sharing Mommy's new diet and refraining from alcohol and junk food not only will make Daddy healthier but will provide much-needed comfort and sympathy to the woman undergoing all the stress, sacrifice, and physical burden of their pregnancy.

On an unrelated topic, **Heineken's new five-liter mini-keg** is easily concealed behind any large leafy vegetable.

CHAPTER 3

Month 1

An Introduction to Existentialism

Your first four weeks in utero are an uncertain time. Your body is changing in strange ways. You are having new experiences, such as **being**, and visiting new places, such as **anywhere**. Just remember: The Chinese character for "crisis" also means "opportunity."* Your coming into being is the chance of a lifetime. So don't feel intimidated. It really is true what they say: "Unicellularity" begins with "you"!

Best Weeks Ever! 1–4

WEEK 1

Sorry to begin the week-by-week wrap-up with such bad news, but here goes: You only have two weeks to not live. No, seriously:

---

* And "onion." And "blithely." And "Yemen." There are only five characters in the Chinese language.

You won't officially be alive for two more weeks. Why? Because the boneheads "out there" (*you* know who we're talking about) have no clue when in the month you were actually conceived. So they mark you down as beginning at the start of Week 3. Essentially, you acted now, and they threw in the first fourteen days as a bonus just for signing up!

WEEK 2

You still don't exist, so your schedule looks pretty open. But Mommy's keeping herself very busy: Her **uterus** is thickening, her **follicles** are maturing, and her **ability to look at other people's babies without tearing up** is deteriorating by the minute. At some point near the end of this week, Mommy and Daddy will engage in the sex act that will create you. If they're randy, they may also engage in a few other sex acts that can't create anybody.

WEEK 3

The coolest, craziest, most batshit insane week of your whole fetalcy. Some of what's happening we discussed in the Conception chapter; we'll discuss more of it in this one. For now, the main point to stress is: *Pace yourself.* As eager as you are to get started, it's just not realistic to expect to reach your full growth potential in a week or even a month. If you start acting a little crazy now, within a few days you'll be totally zygotic.

WEEK 4

Our first juicy piece of gossip: Looks like it's splitsville for **you** and **the half of you that will become the placenta**! Tough break. Here's hoping they stay close for the sake of the child. Anyway, this is a good week to— Oh no! Now your **endoderm,**

mesoderm, and **ectoderm** are splitting up? Wait a second—you mean the three of them were living together in the first place?! Yowzers! It really *is* another world in there, isn't it?

What You May Be Concerned She's Not Concerned About

THE YOU NOBODY KNOWS

"Sometimes I think my parents don't even know I exist!"

They probably don't. Depending on how health-conscious she is and how truly "expected" you were, Mommy may not be aware of your presence for weeks, months, or even—in the case of those overweight women you sometimes read about who think they've had gas or stomach pains for nine months until next thing they know they're in the hospital claiming they have food poisoning *but surprise, surprise! You were in labor, you moron!*—the entire pregnancy.

In the majority of cases, Mommy will begin to suspect something a few days after she misses her period. She will then notify Daddy, who, depending on his attitude toward fatherhood, may *also* miss her period. They will then head to the

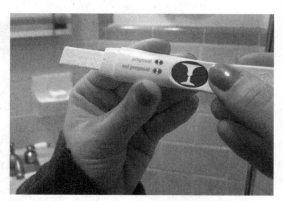

Fig. 15. *A typical home pregnancy test. After immersion in urine, the appearance of two faces will indicate pregnancy; a vase, no pregnancy.*

drugstore to buy a **home pregnancy test** (Fig. 15). In the old days such tests were crude and untrustworthy and took about a

"How Do You Make a Hormone?"

Everyone knows the answer to *that* old chestnut: "Through a complex process of biosynthesis!" And HCG is only one of the kooky kemicals Mommy will be producing during your stay in the womb.

HUMAN CHORIONIC GONADOTROPIN (HCG)

What it does: Ensures secretion of large amounts of progesterone at the beginning of fetalcy

What it does to Mommy: Ensures secretion of large amounts of tears at start of Keira Knightley's latest schlockfest

HUMAN PLACENTAL LACTOGEN (HPL)

What it does: Modifies metabolism, decreasing insulin sensitivity and freeing glucose for use as rapid energy

What it does to Mommy: Modifies personality, increasing emotional sensitivity and freeing old resentments for use in rabid arguments

year. But today's versions are extremely reliable, and anxious would-be parents can place great confidence in such leading brands as E-Z-P, Accu-Pee, Leak 'n' Peek, Flow 'n' Know, and Carl Yastrzemski's Polish-Style Home Pregnancy Test with Kielbasa. They all work by detecting the presence of **HCG**, a hormone (see chart) found only in Chinese food and the urine of pregnant women.

Even without the pee stick, Mommy will probably catch on pretty quickly, because the beginning of pregnancy usually

ESTROGEN

What it does: Regulates progesterone, aiding development of sexual characteristics, promoting blood flow in uterus

What it does to Mommy: Regulates—oh, what does it matter? Life is endless sorrow. [*Pause; uncontrollable sobbing.*]

PROGESTERONE

What it does: Readies uterus for implantation by decreasing immune response

What it does to Mommy: Shut. The. Fuck. Up. Now.

PROLACTIN

What it does: Prepares Mommy's breasts for lactation

What it does to Mommy: Shut. Up. And. Fuck. Me. Now.

comes with telltale signs. Among them: **swollen or tender breasts**; **cramps**; **sudden weight gain of .000004 pounds**; **profound happiness and/or nausea**; **self-identification with Ishtar, the Babylonian earth goddess**; **a visceral awareness of entering into the most mysterious and beautiful of all human experiences**; and **constipation**.

As for notifying the general public, that might take even longer. For every woman who announces her pregnancy to the world through a press release issued from the drugstore bathroom, there are ten who opt *not* to notify friends and loved ones until the third month has passed. So be patient. The news *will* get out, the wire services *will* pick it up, and your fifteen minutes *will* come and go long before you're born.

LOCATION, LOCATION, LOCATION

"I know I live in Mommy, but am I in one of her nicer neighborhoods?"

The nicest! You're in the glamorous **ObGyn section** of beautiful downtown Mom. You're currently staying in one of her two **Fallopian tubes**, named for Renaissance anatomist Gabriel Falloppius, their inventor (Fig. 16). The tubes are worth a quick visit; the **fimbriae** are particularly attractive. (Open Mon.–Fri. 8 A.M.–4 P.M.; $8, free for 0 and under). But savvy zygotes know the real excitement begins with the journey to the **uterus**: A three-day Venetian-style cruise with your cell wall as gondola, the ciliae as your gondoliers, and the distant rumblings of bowel movements as your romantic *barcarole*. This will be your new home. As befitting someone of your importance, it's located between the bladder and the rectum.* It's cramped but provides room and board and is overall as comfortable a living space as you're likely to find inside another person. Congratulations—in less than five days, you've entered a part of Mommy that Daddy probably didn't reach for weeks!

Fig. 16. *Gabriel Falloppius. He also gave his name to falloppini, a noodle shaped like a labia.*

---

* A.k.a. "BlaRec."

DUE AND DON'T

"How long am I gonna be cooped up in here? I'm sixteen cells big and ready to take on the world!"

Slow down, kiddo! You've got spunk, all right, but there's still the little matter of the **one or two trillion more cells** you're going to need before you can hit the big ze-ro. It's a process called **gestation**, and its length varies widely among species, anywhere from five minutes (*Alien*) to untold thousands of years (*The Thing*). In the case of *Homo sapiens,* gestation lasts around **forty weeks**. This period is traditionally divided into **three trimesters**, and it is strongly recommended that you follow them *in order.* If all goes well, figure to be here around nine months. If you were conceived on New Year's Eve, you should be able to catch the World Series. If you were conceived on Valentine's Day, you might just keep Mom from voting. If you were conceived on Memorial Day . . . well, that's very disrespectful.

> **UTERINE LINER NOTE**
>
> *"Whenever I'm in the uterus, I like to implant myself in the **endometrium**. Not only is it **predecidualized** for my convenience, it has **pinopodes** with **macromolecules** and **underlying basal lamina** that are perfect for my **trophoblasts**. And you can't beat the location!"*
>
> —Week 8, Flint, Michigan

But you want to know *exactly* when, don't you, you little control freak you! Well, at some point in the next few months, you'll overhear the doctor giving Mommy her **due date**. You may interpret this as their passive-aggressive way of nagging you to be on time. You're right. But here's a little secret they don't want you to know: *Less than 5 percent of babies are actually born on their due date,* and most of them grow up to be accountants. So you do have a little wiggle room.*

---

* You're living in it.

GREAT. EXPECTATIONS.

"I'm only sixty-four cells big. How am I ever going to grow into a fully formed human being?"

(Author's note: This question will be guest-answered by one of the world's leading motivational speakers and authors, Dr. Phil McGraw.)

You're "how"-ing yourself "no" before "yes" gets its shoes on!

Here's a little secret, okay. Nobody ever got to where they are now by worrying about where they'd be when they were then. You're starting off at the same place everybody else started, which is at the beginning. And by the time you're done, you'll arrive at the same ending everybody else arrives at, and guess what? By the time that ending's over, it's finished and everything's done.

So the question becomes: Are you gonna get there making excuses, or are you gonna get there making sausage?

Now, I understand hesitation, and I understand fear. We're human beings, and that means we make mistakes, and that means we're fallible, and that means we're imperfect; bearing blemish; defective or inadequate. So it's not a matter of whether or not there's some part of you that's rotten, because there is. The point is, is it that there's a part of you that's rotten, or is it that there's a part of what's rotten that's you? And that's something only you and the rottenness can answer.

Now, I'm gonna check back in with you in a few months to see how you're making out, okay? And here's what I'm hoping we're gonna see: a mature, responsible ten-week fetus that's holding himself to account for what he's doing with his life.

Is that what we're gonna see? We'll find out next time.

You're Two Much

"AAAAAAAHHHHH who the fuck is that!?"

Your **twin**.

Sometimes, when a mommy and daddy love each other twice as much as other mommies and daddies, their sperm and egg get together to make *two* babies. The pair then develop and grow together, sharing the same amount of love that would have gone to just one of them if the other one didn't exist.

There are two kinds of twin, just as there are eight kinds of octopi and a thousand kinds of millipedes. **Fraternal twins** come from two separate eggs that attach themselves to the uterine wall, making them **dizygotic**, or **biovular**, or **hemi-quadrafertilistic-eggs-be-in-a-fetus**. Genetically, they are no more alike than any other siblings. They may be born different genders, or even as fans of different professional hockey teams. **Identical twins**, on the other hand, are formed when a single fertilized egg splits into two embryos. Since their DNA is the same, they will look exactly alike, and their lucky parents are free to let Hollywood producers exploit them in a clever circumvention of child-labor laws.

From Mommy's standpoint, a twin pregnancy means more doctor's visits and more potential for nausea, weight gain, and insomnia. So she gets off easy. For you, sharing a womb with a parasitic doppelgänger presents more daunting challenges:

- **Positioning.** The baby closer to the cervix is called "Baby A." The one farther away is "Baby B." Nobody wants to be

> **UTERINE LINER NOTE**
>
> *"The doctor told me I was due 7 Muluc 12 Yax, but I came out nearly two weeks late—on 6 Etznab 16 Mac!"*
>
>
>
> —Itzel Shogiuchilou, Chichén Itzá, Mexico, c. AD 1450

Famous Twins

Many twins have grown up to be famous. A few have even done so without posing naked.

Ross and Norris McWhirter created *The Guinness Book of Records,* setting a new world record for most books of world records created (1).

Born Esther and Pauline Friedman, **Ann Landers and Abigail Van Buren** grew rich dispensing good advice. The best advice they ever got? "Ditch the 'Friedman.' "

Mary-Kate and Ashley Olsen's parents are Bob Saget, John Stamos, and the guy Alanis Morissette wrote "You Oughta Know" about. In 1995 they died, leaving the Olsens $24 billion, which they used to kill Heath Ledger.

The vagueness of parody laws, and their pertinence to public figures, leaves it unclear as to whether **Jenna and Barbara Bush** can be referred to in print as filthy drunks.

Superheroes who respectively transformed into animals or forms of water, the **Wonder Twins** were named for their ability to make people "wonder" what the fuck retard came up with them.

Chang and Archie Bunker, the original "Siamese twins," lived a rich and a happy life, despite Archie's constant complaints about Chang being "a slant-eyed rice-eater."

Romulus and Remus, co-founders of Rome, were raised by a she-wolf, overcoming the stigma associated with single-wolf families.

Luke Skywalker and Princess Leia Organa, the central characters of the *Star Wars* films, were the twin children of Darth Vader and Lando Calrissian.

The need for **Gunnar and Matthew Nelson** to round off this list reveals the surprisingly small number of famous twins.

the B-baby. B-babies are losers. B-babies are destined for second place. Wriggle, writhe, squirm, lie, steal—*do whatever it takes* to out-cervix your sibling. Be an A-baby . . . or B-nobody.

- **Socializing.** It can be awkward spending the better part of a year stuck in close quarters with someone who is not only a potential rival but not much of a conversationalist. It's probably best to pass the time in silence. If you do make small talk, try to limit it to general topics. The weather is usually a safe subject, as it is always the same.

- **Individuation.** Particularly important for *identical* twins. Go out of your way to distinguish yourself from your wombmate. If she's not much of a kicker, kick. If she likes to stretch, stay still. If she likes you, hate her. Forge your own personality now . . . while you still can. As you will one day discover, gestation will be the last time in many years you and your identical twin won't be made to dress in matching "Double Trouble" rabbit-ear onesies that render you gallingly interchangeable.

Identical Twins!

Sharing this copy of *What® to Expect When You're® Expected*? Why not order another! Already have two? Then buy a third and fight over it!

Multiples

"There are actually two other babies in here with me. Is it possible that—"

You know, stop right there, because now it's just getting ridiculous, all right? *Three?* Really? Is that what it's come to now? Enough.

Fig. 17. *Seriously, is your mother a pig?*

A Fetal Examination®
MOMMY'S BEAUTY REGIMEN: PREGNANCY'S TOP PRIORITY

Face it: If you're going to be seen in public with Mom for the next nine months, you don't want her to look all, you know, *pregnant*. Mommy's appearance reflects on you. When people see a mother who's let her looks go to pot, it's natural for them to assume her unborn baby is similarly unkempt. Before you know it, the whole neighborhood is talking about Mrs. Uglymommy and her slovenly, slovenly embryo.

Beauty is in the eye of the beholder, and since Mommy be holding you, she has the final say in matters of beauty. But there are a few things you both need to know about pregnancy and style.

Hair

+ **Oh no! The fuzz!** Mommy will be sprouting more hair in places she already has it (armpits, bikini line) and new hair in places she doesn't (ears, lungs). Shaving or plucking is fine, but she might want to consider giving you a leg up on childbirth with a "pregnancy wax."

+ **Dye, Mommy, dye.** We're not saying that Mommy colors her hair. (Eye roll.) But if she *did,* it should be safe for her to keep doing it all through pregnancy.* Note: Some experts are more cautious and recommend that she use less intense, half-strength coloring products, such as the just-released Alberto VO2½.

+ **When perms meet egg.** Though chemically safe, perms won't work on Mommy because of pregnancy's unpredictable impact on hair's body, volume, luster, gloss, radiance, shine, sheen, shoon, bounce, spring, silkience, satinence, chiffonosity, manageability, work ethic, overall outlook on life, and earned run average.

FACE

+ **Don't feed the pore.** Facials are safe. Just try not to schedule one with that Yukio girl. She never shuts up.

+ **A pimple plan.** Pregnancy acne is quite common. It's best treated with fifty to one hundred rigorous scrubs daily of either an exfoliant (such as Olay) or defoliant (such as Agent Orange). Otherwise, Mommy might start looking like she did in high school . . . you know, the last time she was pregnant.

+ **Lipstick on a piglet.** Pregnancy's various skin discolorations (see Month 5) can be treated with any makeup that's "noncomedogenic," or "not funny." Mommy can use products like foundation, eyeliner, and mascara without guilt, because they've been rigorously tested for decades on untold millions of small adorable pregnant animals.

---

* Assuming she's not a stickler for complete "curtain/drape concordance," if you know what we mean.

BODY

- **Scents of purpose.** As long as she avoids certain oils, Mommy can take aromatherapy. P.S.: Her upcoming gassiness means Daddy can look forward to many free sessions of aromasuffering.
- **Brown out.** No tanning beds—they're too hot. No prolonged exposure to the sun—it can cause melanoma. And no tanning sprays—she'll look like an anemic clementine.
- **Manicure and pedicure.** Perfectly safe. Mommy can walk right in and start—oh, shit. It's Yukio.

CHAPTER 4

Month 2

Making Mitosis *Your*tosis

During Weeks 5–8 of your fetalcy, you'll grow more recognizably human, even as Mommy's behavior grows ever less so. Parts of your body will start to specialize. A corporate hierarchy will begin developing inside you. By the end of the month, you'll be an enormous organization, thriving in an environment many would find hostile. What began as a tiny mom-and-pop operation is now a uterine Wal-Mart, swallowing up ever greater quantities of natural resources in its insatiable desire to grow bigger.

Best Weeks Ever! 5–8

WEEK 5

It's a big milestone for you: You're now large enough to be compared with various pieces of fruit. (We've provided a chart on the next page.) Even better, you now have a **heartbeat**. Yes, it's a

A GROWTH CHART: YOU VS. PRODUCE

AT WEEK NUMBER . . .	YOU CAN . . .
5	pummel a pomegranate seed
6	choke a chokecherry
7	batter a blueberry
8	roughhouse a raspberry
9	grapple a grape
10	flog a fig
11	lay into a lime
12	plunk a plum
13	beat the fucking shit out of a peach

very, very faint heartbeat, but many great things start out that way. (For example, Pink Floyd's *Dark Side of the Moon*.) But the tadpole thing . . . it isn't really working. And maybe get rid of that tail. It's taking us back . . . waaaaay too far back.

WEEK 6

You're really cooking now: **lungs**, **liver**, **kidneys**. Your **jaws**, **cheeks**, and **chin** are starting to take shape too, although to be honest, at this point your features are not your best features. But it's okay—you're just laying the groundwork. Those two black dots? **Eyes**. Those two side holes? **Ears**. Those two shiny things at the bottom of the holes? **Piercings**. Schweeeeet!

WEEK 7

You're getting new **brain cells** at the rate of one hundred a minute. That's great. Just remember, brains aren't everything. There's also a little something called street smarts, and guess what, partner? You ain't got none! . . . Sorry. Uncalled for. Seriously, your brain is very impressive, and we're also very impressed with those **arm and leg buds** you've sprouted, although you'll forgive us if we don't give you a celebratory Rolex just yet.

WEEK 8

Your **lips** are forming and your **eyelids** are taking shape. The tip of your **nose** is apparent and your **ears** are clearly recognizable. Plus, your arm and leg buds have differentiated into distinct segments. To recap: You have a rudimentary head, shoulders, knees, and toes. A rudimentary head, shoulders, knees, and toes. Rudimentary eyes, and ears, and mouth, and nose. Rudimentary head, shoulders, knees, and toes.*

What You May Be Concerned She's Not Concerned About

STAIRWAY TO HEAVIN'

"Why is Mommy throwing up all the time?"

Short answer: You make her sick.

Long answer: She's suffering from a condition called **morning sickness**, or, as it's known to pregnant bulimics, **morning**. In

---

* Knees and toes.

Get to Know Your Organs

It seems every day of your first trimester brings another fun new body part or system to play with. You'll feel like a kid in a kid shop! But getting so many new toys so quickly can be overwhelming. Before you know it, you're in over your head, confused, trying to breathe through your heart and think with your pancreas. Most fetuses figure out what's what after a little trial and error, but here's a brief overview to help you get started:

Organ: Brain

A.k.a.: The Cogitator; Ol' Thinky; Zombie Pie

Description: Wrinkly, turtle-shaped sponge in upper head

Functions: Doing all your thinking, or, if you're a boy, almost half of it; also useful for forming your personality, making intuitive leaps, holding grudges, and inexplicably remembering the sax solo from Quarterflash's 1982 hit "Harden My Heart"

Tidbit: You are currently using your brain to process this tidbit.

Organ: Ears

A.k.a.: Hear and There; Sound and Fury; Vincent van Goghnads

Description: Two large, flesh-colored *orecchiette*

Functions: Receiving sonic information (one ear); releasing sonic information (other)

Tidbit: "To be deaf is a greater affliction than to be blind." —Helen Keller, the world's least-qualified person to make that assessment

Organ:	Eyes
A.k.a.:	Peepers; Lookholes; Mr. and Mrs. Seestuff
Description:	White spheres with concentric circles (Note: May be hard to see without mirror)
Function:	Watching TV
Tidbit:	Most people use only 10 percent of their eyes. The other eighteen eyes just sit there doing nothing.

Organ:	Nose
A.k.a.:	Stinky; Ol' Smelly; Julius Sneezer
Description:	Dual-site open-pit central-face mucus mine
Functions:	Breathing; instantly taking you back to that summer on the lake in Vermont; Jew-distinguishing
Tidbit:	Go ahead. Everyone does. Start with your pinky.

Organ:	Mouth
A.k.a.:	The Kisser; the Nicknamer; the North End of the Stinkin' Tunnel
Description:	Large hole in face that moves unconsciously when you read
Functions:	Eating; talking; overeating; talking too much
Tidbit:	The mouth is the nine-time winner of the AMA's Most Valuable Orifice Award, second only to the anus (11).

Body part:	Skeleton
A.k.a.:	Bones; Darth Ritis; Mr. Tibia (*"They call me Mr. Tibia!"*)
Description:	All that really hard white stuff that keeps banging into things

Body part: Skeleton (*cont.*)

Function: Corrects your posture

Tidbit: While all adults have 206 bones in their bodies, a handful keep even *more* bones in their refrigerator/freezer.

Organ: Heart

A.k.a.: The Ticker; Pump 'n' Dump; Ba-Dum-Bum-(*rim shot*)

Description: Red, pulsing, and surprisingly not all that heart-shaped

Functions: Pumping blood throughout body; regulating circulatory system; breaking; getting chewed up, spit out, trampled on, shot through, etc.

Tidbit: Though a social fisherman and a gregarious hiker, the heart is a lonely hunter.

Body part: Arms/hands

A.k.a.: Huggers; Hitchers; The Shoulders That Went Too Far

Description: Two long tubes on side of torso ending in turkey-shaped outcropping

Functions: Grabbing, holding, intentional grounding, offensive pass interference

Tidbit: One of the key developments in the evolution of man was the creation of the opposable thumb by God on Day 6.

Organ: Liver

A.k.a.: Al Coholic; Sir Osis; Tony Absorbsalotofbooze

Description: Pinkish brown, football-sized, choppable

Functions: Performs five hundred different jobs, from glycogenesis to protein metabolism to Web design

Tidbit: Controversially, many of those jobs are now being performed by illegal Mexican immigrant livers.

Organ: Kidneys

A.k.a.:   Billy the Kidneys

Description: Reddish brown, shaped like bean and/or small backyard swimming pool

Function: Filters and stores urine for excretion and later use in Ayurvedic mimosas

Tidbit: Human beings can live with only one kidney, but nobody knows which one.

Organ: Genitals

A.k.a.:   There ain't enough ink to print 'em

Description: Ummm . . . well, they're a little . . .
                Remember at the zoo, when we saw . . .
                Ask your mother.

Function: Hopefully

Tidbit: (Boy fetuses only) Your penis is much, much smaller than other men's.

Body Part: Legs

A.k.a.:   Gams, Kneetwigs, Greco-Roman Wrestling Non-factors

Description: Like arms, but feetier

Functions: Walking, running, pogo sticking, hailing taxis

Tidbit: To earn the approbation of ZZ Top, the mere having of legs is, for a woman, insufficient; rather, she must also be adroit in their proper utilization.

Fig. 18. *The miracle that is you makes your mother vomit.*

truth, the name is a double misnomer—not only can its symptoms strike at any and all hours, but as the daily result of a voluntary condition, it is technically not a sickness but a lifestyle choice (Fig. 18). Nevertheless, well over half of new mothers experience some form of the disorder, and those who don't can (and should) feel very guilty about it and make themselves carsick once a week just for form's sake.

The causes of morning sickness remain shrouded in vomit. One theory suggests the brain's normal nausea catalysts become overstimulated by Mommy's new hypersensitivity to odors, which may explain its high incidence among sewer workers and dungsmiths. Others suggest it was an evolutionary means of keeping mothers from foods harmful to the embryo, Nature's way of telling cavewomen, "Mud no baby yum-yum." Sigmund Freud even suggested that morning sickness was a manifestation of a mother's repressed hatred for her husband. Then again, Freud's overall bag was sucking the fun out of life like jelly from a donut.

From your standpoint, Mommy's morning sickness should be seen as a throw-upportunity. It's a chance to set

> **UTERINE LINER NOTE**
>
> *"My mother threw up every morning at 11:00 A.M. It was so funny! It got to the point that I'd hear her puking and say to my twin, 'Wonder who's on* The View *today!'"*
>
> —Week 18, Boise, Idaho

an important precedent: For the next eighteen years, *you* will have the power to turn her insides out and make her miserable. Alas, even your most concerted efforts probably won't be enough to sustain her suffering past the first trimester. Besides, over the years women have adopted strategies to deal with morning sickness:

- **Drinking fluids.** Easier than eating them.
- **Avoiding odors.** As mentioned, pregnant women's sense of smell is remarkable. In clinical tests, some have been able to detect the presence of a single clove of garlic in Lake Ontario.
- **Sea-Bands.** Elastic bands worn on the wrists. Also used to combat seasickness. Pregnant women on fishing boats are advised to wear multiple pairs, and also not to have done something as stupid as going out on a fishing boat.
- **Taking it easy in the morning.** Smart mommies don't bolt out of bed for work. Rather, they snooze for twenty minutes. Then twenty more. Then another hour. Then call in sick. Then *Ellen.* Whew! Nap time.

- **Ginger.** The reason for ginger's remarkable effectiveness in soothing upset stomachs is unknown, though scientists suspect it may have something to do with Schweppervescence.
- **Alternative medicine.** Includes acupuncture, acupressure, biofeedback, and laughter, which after all is the best medicine, except for actual medicine.

Fig. 19. *Antonio Banderas's roles have spanned a broad variety of styles, from family comedy to intense drama.*

And of course, there's one thing pregnant women should definitely *not* do if they're looking to avoid feeling weak in the knees: stare at pictures of scintillating Spaniard **Antonio Banderas** (Fig. 19)!

THE RETCHER IN THE GUY

"Why is Daddy throwing up all the time?"

Short answer: He's a pussy.

Long answer: He's suffering from a condition called "sympathetic pregnancy" or, as it's known in the international *language* of pussies, **couvade**. Its symptoms can mimic nearly everything Mommy is going through—not just morning sickness but weight gain, constipation, leg cramps, and in extreme cases vaginal bleeding.

The causes of couvade remain shrouded in imitation vomit. What is the underlying emotion at work? Anxiety? Rage? Cowardice? Is Daddy jealous that only mommies get to carry babies? If so, is he also jealous that only plants get to perform photosynthesis? Or does he think the pity routine will somehow score him points with the old lady? Because that doesn't make a lick of sense. You think Mommy wants to look up from her toilet to see Daddy puking in the sink like *he's* got an excuse?

This is the part where we're supposed to tell you couvade is normal and suggest ways Daddy can relieve his symptoms and blah blah blah, but honestly? The guy's got to man up. Yes, he can be nervous and exultant and scared and unsure, and by all means he should help Mommy however he can. But clenching his stomach because he suddenly "felt the baby kick" is not helping—it is infuriating. If Mommy's smart, she'll set him straight. If he's too "sick" to have sex, she should shame him by claiming he's giving her "a case of blue balls."

FATIGUE

"Why is Mommy always tired? I've never felt so alive!"

Puzzling, isn't it? Here you are, full of energy, busy trying to create a life for yourself, working 24/7/280, yet *she's* the one always complaining about being tired, as if some "mysterious creature" no one else could see was "draining her body" and "sucking her life force."

But to be fair, mothers do play a subtle (though not essential) role in an embryo's early development. For starters, there's the matter of your **placenta**, your personalized—and in rare cases monogrammed—carrying case. Creating a placenta requires a great deal of energy, particularly if Mom loves you enough to spring for a quality placenta, because let's be honest, there are a lot of shoddy placentas out there.* The first trimester also brings many other physical and emotional stresses that tax Mommy's body and force Daddy to do things he may never have done before, like shop for groceries, or listen, or help.

Chances are Mommy will be taking it a little easy these first three months, going to bed earlier, waking up later, canceling all but her most essential triathlons. Dishes may go unwashed. This is normal. The dishes may start to pile up. Again, normal. The household's entire collection of cookware may soon form a giant game of Jenga in the sink that stands in silent condemnation of Daddy's astounding selfishness. Par for the course! The important thing is that your mother is getting her rest, and that *her* mother is getting to see the kind of man her daughter really married.

---

* You know the ones, where the trophoblast leaks and the syncytiotrophoblast might as well be made out of balsa wood and the contractors are all in the Placenta Builders' Union, so *they* could give a shit.

PEEING AND NOTHINGNESS

"Again with the bathroom?"

Frequent urination is one of the most common side effects of pregnancy, and one your mother can do very little about. So she and her pregnant friends may as well turn it into something fun with one of the following **peeing games**.

- **Quarters.** Attempt to bounce a quarter off a hard surface into a shot glass. When successful, pee.
- **Beer pong.** Place plastic cups full of beer on either side of a Ping-Pong table. When she hits the ball into her opponent's cup . . . well, she can't drink, obviously. She's pregnant. But she can pee.
- **Bullshit.** Players sit in a circle talking about what an unmitigated joy it is to be pregnant. Bullshit. Everybody pees.
- **I Never.** Players go around in a circle telling each other things they've never done, and will never have a chance to now that you're pregnant. Sob. Pee.

A Fetal Examination®
PREGNANCY AND WORK: JOB/GYN

UTERINE LINER NOTE

"Mommy has a job as a human cannonball. By my third trimester she had to grease the cannon."

—David B., age two months,
Wilkes-Barre, Pennsylvania

Strange but true: A small but growing number of women have chosen to join their stronger, less moody male counterparts in the field of wage earning. Today's female job holder, or "workrix," contributes much to society, be she a schoolmarm, secretary of state, or laundress. But pregnant women often have concerns about navigating their way through the world of nine-to-five, especially during Months 5 to 9.

WORKPLACE SAFETY

Office work. Because it is so unrewarding, office work is extremely safe. The notion that prolonged time at a computer terminal may expose the unborn to harmful radiation has been scientifically proven to be a myth spread by **that asshole Phil in marketing**. Physically, office work deals pregnant women very few hardships and a great many softships. To be on the safe side, Mommy should **take frequent breaks** from sitting; **stretch** frequently; and, to the extent possible, avoid **that asshole Phil in marketing** (Fig. 20). But for the most part, Mommy can probably keep working until the start of the "maternity leave" she believes will last three months but will in fact, through the gradual acceptance of her own loss of professional identity, last the rest of her life.

Fig. 20. *That asshole Phil in marketing.*

Health-care work. This can be risky for pregnant women, although on the plus side, if something goes wrong, there are lots of **health-care workers** around. Among the dangers for hospital employees are chemicals like **formaldehyde**,* along with exposure to **infection**, **radiation**, and **enough human misery to make any woman wonder what kind of sick world her child is being born into**.

* A more casual option: **semi-formaldehyde**.

Manufacturing work. The threat here is to neither you nor Mommy but the American economy. Let's be blunt: There are women overseas willing to do the same jobs twice as pregnant and for half the pay. How can American textile companies hope to compete when pregnant Malaysian sweatshop workers will sew jeans for $1.50 an hour—*and* keep stitching through labor?

Physically stressful work. If Mommy has a physically grueling job involving heavy lifting or operating large pieces of machinery, she should request an early maternity leave, so that she and her lesbian partner can focus exclusively on the pregnancy.

OFFICE POLITICS

For her **co-workers**, Mommy's pregnancy is sure to unleash a welter of conflicting emotions (Fig. 21). Are they happy for her? Absolutely, kind of. But now they know that every morning brings them one step closer to the day they're asked to "tem-

Fig. 21.

porarily" take on some of her crappy-ass duties. And even before that moment arrives, the sight of her growing belly will serve as a constant reminder that she has a life outside the office, a fact that in and of itself will elicit tremendous jealousy from most of her colleagues.

Then there's **Mommy's boss** (see Fig. 22). He had a lot of faith in her. He

Fig. 22. *Mommy's boss.*

thought this company meant *everything* to her. Now this is the thanks he gets for choosing her over **that asshole Phil in sales** (Fig. 23)? "Yes, I hereby grant you your 'maternity leave,' as in 'Maternity?! *Leave!*' "

ig. 23. *Apparently they transferred that sshole Phil over to sales.*

The protocol of such situations can be tricky, particularly if Mommy is at a point in her career where *her* office space is not much bigger than *yours*. But when breaking the news, she should definitely tell her boss *first,* so he won't hear about it from the office gossip—which ironically, under any other circumstance, would be her. Timing is also critical; if she isn't showing yet, she might want to wait and demonstrate her loyalty with one more headfirst slide at the company softball game. When the moment is right, she should schedule an appointment, come into the meeting with a plan and a positive attitude, be responsive, listen to his concerns, then quickly and efficiently pack up her belongings. (Just kidding! Mommy is afforded legal protection by 1978's **Pregnancy Discrimination Act**, which makes it a crime to fire a pregnant woman even if her previous children came out ugly.)

In general, Mommy should broach the subject of her pregnancy to her boss with honesty and candor. The only exception is if she is married but he is the father. In that case, the wisest course is a mutual pact of eternal, anguished silence.

If Mommy is lucky enough to *be* the boss, she has more options in announcing her happy news. A simple memo may suffice.

To: Acme Widgets, Inc.
From: Jane Newmother, CEO
Date: January 12, 2009
Re: Personnel announcement

In synergy with my partner, I have decided to launch
a horizontal-expansion project to enhance our human
resources. The project will culminate in a deliver-
able that is expected to push my envelope (via a
strategic gap) outside the box. Our best guessti-
mate as to the project's unveiling date is early
October, as it was first run up his flagpole back in
mid-December.

At the end of the day, I intend to do most of the
heavy lifting on this one. However, in the short
term, the intrapersonal multitasking involved is
causing me extreme internal pushback. My bottom
line is suffering, and my "toss it against the wall
and see what sticks" approach is evident to anyone
who's visited the women's room lately.

Moving forward, I am confident these first-quarter
setbacks will give way to brisk growth in the second and third, as bandwidth development becomes
more robust. Until then, I am certain that increased
teamworking, coupled with a flexible game plan, will
enable us to navigate these exciting times and turn
what might otherwise be a fire drill into a win-win
or, if it's twins, a win-win-win-win.

Jane

P.S. The topic of baby names is permanently offline.

CHAPTER 5

Month 3
Vaguely Human!

As of Week 9 you're no longer an embryo—you're officially a **fetus**. It's a painful truth, one that may send you
spiraling into a pre-life crisis. Let's face it: You're not the
same innocent, uneyed blastocyst who made his way to the wide,
wide uterus ten weeks ago with little more than a couple of cells
and a whole lot of moxie. Seriously, what *happened* to you, man?
You've changed. It used to be about the growing. Now you're all
about fitting in, looking "normal" for the outside world so they
don't flip out when they see you in pictures.

Best Weeks Ever! 9–13

WEEK 9

See, this is what we're talking about. What's with all the **muscles**,
man?! You *totally* did not have those before. Don't tell me you've
just been working out. You've been bulking up, haven't you?

You're getting that stuff pumped right into you. Come here, let us feel your heart. Come on, let us feel it! Jesus, man, it's **180 beats a minute**! Why are you doing this to yourself? Is it really worth it? 'Cause here's a promise: In six months, when all this is over, you are *not* going to want to look the way you look right now.

WEEK 10

All right, maybe we overreacted. Maybe there's a method to your madness. We didn't realize you were also growing **bones** and **cartilage**. Obviously, that's a more encouraging development. Your **elbows** are bending, too, so flexibility doesn't seem to be an issue. Sorry we doubted you. It wasn't fair to—oh, man. Wait a second. You're producing **testosterone** (if you're a boy) all of a sudden?! We *were* right! You *are* on the juice!

WEEK 11

Okay, listen: If you're on the up-and-up, if you're totally clean, explain your **torso lengthening**. Explain the new **hair follicles**. Explain the **ovaries** (if you're a girl). And explain the way you generally just don't even look like a nonhuman being anymore. We *want* to believe you. We *want* to think this is all happening naturally. But frankly, if it is? It's maybe the greatest miracle in the history of creation.

WEEK 12

Sigh . . . Since we're tired of feeling disillusioned, we're going to stop asking questions and just appreciate you for what you're doing, however you're doing it. Your **digestive system** is starting up. Terrific. Your **bone marrow** is making **white blood cells**. Fantastic. Your **pituitary gland** has started producing **hor-**

mones. Right, like *that's* not a telltale sign of—Jesus. Say it ain't so, fetus. Say it ain't so. [*Walks away in disgust.*]

WEEK 13

You know what? It's the end of the first trimester. Time to start fresh. No matter what's been going on behind the scenes, it's over now. It takes guts to admit you've made a mistake, and judging by the **intestines growing inside your belly**, you've got those guts. So let's just forget this whole thing ever happened, shall we? Great. Something tells us the *second* trimester is going to feel a whole lot better for *everybody*.

What You May Be Concerned She's Not Concerned About

INTESTINAL GROUNDING

"Christ Almighty, what's that stench in here?"

Constipation is one of pregnancy's most common side effects, and unquestionably the one Daddy is least interested in hearing about. Hormonal changes will often cause bowel muscles to relax, making them unable to perform the feces-processing work they love so dearly. Food then winds up taking up lodging in the intestine indefinitely, leading to a backup that can make trips to the bathroom a long, torturous—

Hey! Stop snickering! This is serious, all right? Show some sympathy for Mommy. Not only is she constipated all the time, she has to *think* about being constipated all the time, and that can cause a mental blockage worse than the physical one. Let's be blunt: Adults don't like thinking about shit more than they have to. They've got other, *non*-shit shit to think about. "If that's true," you may say, "why did she choose to have a shit factory like *me*?" Because you don't shit. You *poop*. There's a huge difference. Shit is malodorous undigested waste matter. Poop is angel gravy. Within a few weeks even Daddy will be wiping it up like it's melted toffee.

Anyway, exercise, plenty of liquid, and a daily silo of fiber should help Mommy out. In extreme cases, a doctor may recommend a stool softener. If he does, she should try to avoid the rookie mistake of pouring it *on* the stool *after* she passes it.

GAS

"Sorry to stay in the gutter, but that sound I just heard . . ."

Don't be silly. Women don't fart. Next question.

MA'S SO-CALLED LIFE

"So far Mommy is spending most of her pregnancy in a state of stress, anxiety, and depression. Which one should she focus on?"

There's no right answer to that question. Stress, anxiety, and depression are *all* perfectly good irrational emotions for first-term women to let themselves sink into a state of. It comes down to a matter of taste. **Stress** is the neurosis of choice among women with high-pressure jobs—air-traffic controllers, for example, or Harvey Weinstein's palanquin attendants. It's also a good option for those who enjoy living in denial, holding in their feelings, and forbidding themselves a single moment of relaxation.

Anxiety is a better bet for those with a more creative approach to useless worry. Spurred by thoughts of what could go wrong, their imaginations can run wild as they embark on a months-

Fig. 24. *The AMTTCTHBAEU was built in 1916 by a turtle who found a gold mine in Woodrow Wilson's underpants.*

long tour through the galleries of the American Museum of Things That Could Theoretically Happen But Are Extremely Unlikely (Fig. 24). Finally, while **depression** is often tied to biochemistry, it's also a favorite of fans of sighing and pouting, as well as anyone who prefers her angst free of even a semblance of an actual cause.

Bear in mind, however, that stress, anxiety, and depression are by no means separate entities, but rather form what doctors call "the SAD spectrum." Few first-trimester women are "just" depressed or anxious or stressed. They're usually a rich tapestry of all three. Mood swings, listlessness, loss of appetite, low energy levels—who cares exactly *which* emotion deserves the credit? All that matters at the end of the day is that Mommy can't sleep at the end of the day.

The ABCs of Maternal Discomfort

A book of this size can touch on but a handful of the hundreds of bodily ills Mother Nature may jealously inflict on your far less abstract mother. Herewith, an alphabetical primer of some of the ones we didn't even have room for.

ALLERGIES
Can worsen during pregnancy. Sufferers should stay away from areas that have gathered dust, like the room where they keep the workout equipment.

BREASTS
May become swollen, tender, bumpier, veinier. May grow sullen, moody. May require elaborate support system of cantilevers and flying buttresses.

CARPAL TUNNEL SYNDROME
Swollen tissues press on the nerves of the fingers. Not to be confused with **carpal bridge and tunnel syndrome**, wherein drunken Long Islanders nervily give Manhattanites the finger.

DIARRHEA
Best treated with constipation.

EYE PROBLEMS
Dryness and alterations in corneal shape may lead to decreased visual acuity; by the end of pregnancy, there may be *two* reasons Mommy can't see her own feet when standing.

FOOT PROBLEMS
The loosening up of joints can expand feet a whole shoe size. Out: stiletto heels. In: hollowed-out watermelons.

GENITALS, ACHY

Cause: vulvic varicose veins. Say it ten times fast. It's a lot more fun than getting it once.

HEARTBURN

Burning sensation in esophagus. Foods to avoid include chili, curry, and Ocean Spray's Cran-Chili-Curry® Cocktail.

IRON DEFICIENCY

You know what would probably help remedy this? More iron.

JUST GENERALLY NOT FEELING PARTICULARLY GOOD

What?! It's a widely recognized medical condition that happens to start with J.

KNUCKLE SWELLING

Fluid retention at nighttime may lead to temporary removal of Mommy's wedding ring. Fluid consumption in nightclubs may lead to permanent removal of Daddy's.

LOSS OF APPETITE

You need to eat. She needs to throw up. Does someone smell "sitcom"?! Nope, that's puke.

METALLIC TASTE

Odd penny-like taste in mouth. After one hundred days, may be exchanged for taste of crisp one-dollar bill.

NOSEBLEEDS

Common during pregnancy, especially since Mommy picks it all the time.

ORGASM

For reasons of fetal health, sometimes banned during pregnancy . . . like *your* daddy could give a shit.

Make Every Date a Bad Date!

To learn more about the 365 physical ordeals you're subjecting Mom to, pick up a What® to Expect When You're® Expected Malady-a-Day Calendar. September is Viscous Discharge Month!

PRURITIC URTICARIAL PAPULES AND PLAQUES OF PREGNANCY (PUPPP)

So called because women with itchy eczematous blisters popping out of their stretch marks feel better knowing their condition has an adorable acronym.

QUICKENING

The first time Mommy feels a living creature stirring inside her. "That's not a bad thing," you say. No it isn't . . . *unless it's not a baby!*

RESTLESS LEG SYNDROME

Often accompanied by Impatient Knee Disease and Yearnin'-for-Something-Better Ankle Disorder.

SPIDER VEINS

Spider veins. Spider veins. Caused by hormones and blood-flow gains. On your hips. On your thighs. Quite unsightly in shape and size. Look out—here come spider veins.

TEETH AND GUMS

Gingivitis; bleeding gums; teeth loose in sockets. Best to consult with dentist, a.k.a. "a gynecologist of the head."

URINE, EXCESS SUGAR IN

Yes, it tastes better—but at what cost?

VARICOSE VEINS

More severe than spider veins. Sufferers should buy or borrow support pantyhose. Ask Daddy—he keeps some in his sock drawer. Oops!

WARP, SPACE-TIME

Slight increase in the force of gravity due to bending of space-time continuum around thin pregnant woman's belly. Postulated by Albert Einstein; proven by Nicole Richie.

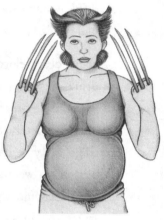

X-MEN SYNDROME

Occurs in 1 to 2 percent of all pregnant women (Fig. 25).

Fig. 25.

YEAST INFECTION

During Passover, must be replaced with matzoh infection.

ZAPF DINGBATS

❖✱✳✴▼✐⬧❖✱❖✳ ▢✱▢✳✴■▼ ▢✳ ▼✳✴▢✳✍▼▢✳○✳▲▼✳▢ ▶▢○✱■ ✳❖■ ▢■●◆ ▼▢▢✳ ✳■ ▼✳✴▲ ▢✳✳✳✱◆●▢◆▲ ✳▢■▼✎

SCALE OF INJUSTICE

"How much total weight gain should I expect?"

Weight gain is an obsession fretted over incessantly throughout these nine months, and for no good reason. *Of course* there's going to be weight gain. You're growing from an embryo to a full-term baby! If you gain seven, eight, even ten pounds between now and delivery, you're right on track and have nothing to worry about.

Wait, were you talking about Mommy? Oh. Yeah, well *she* has

Ask an Old Wife

Q: Is it true that if Mommy doesn't drink enough water, my amniotic fluid will get dirty?

A: O dear beloved Antioch yes! If she drinks anything less than two gallons a day, the dirt-motes will besmirch your sac-jelly faster than you can say "vitiligo"! My neighbor Gertrude failed to wetten her womb but one time her entire fruitfulness, and her poor baby Zebulun was born Negroid! If your mother thirsts not for water, she must provide filtering for your bag-humours by means of a ginger-root suppository grown within the dawn-time shadow of a mandrake root!

Thanks for thy question!

a lot to worry about in this department. This is a fretter. This is one she should obsess over incessantly throughout these nine months.

For first-time mothers, pregnancy raises a host of, shall we say, "substantial" questions.* "How much should I gain? At what rate? If dropped into the Dead Sea, would I still float? Can a larger unit of weight than the pound be used so that the gain can be expressed with a smaller number? Will my body ever return to the way it was before this . . . *incident*?!"

Let's start with total increase. Given the large variety of pre-pregnancy starting points, assigning a single "ideal" weight gain for all women is very difficult. But not impossible. It's thirty-two

---

* In retrospect, the word in quotes should have been "weighty." That would have been cleverer.

pounds. A small-boned size zero may gain as little as thirty-one and a quarter pounds; a larger woman may gain as much as thirty-three. But the target weight is thirty-two pounds on the button, and it is broken down as follows:

Breakdown of Mommy's Weight Gain

(All weights are exact and apply to your Mommy specifically)

Baby	$7^1/_2$ pounds
Bathwater	Negligible
Bazongas	4 pounds
Saddlebags	2 pounds
Muffin tops	2 pounds
Cottage cheese thighs	$2^1/_4$ pounds
Ricotta ass	$2^3/_4$ pounds
Hippo neck	$1^1/_4$ pounds
Walrus scalp	$1^1/_4$ pounds
Camel toes (actually in toes)	1 pound
Udders	8 pounds
Total Weight Gain	*32 pounds*

While Mommy's target weight gain is exact and unchanging, she does have much greater freedom regarding the **rate** of that gain. Basically, as long as she's thirty-two pounds over her prepregnancy weight at the moment she squeezes you out, she's free to add or subtract those pounds anytime she sees fit. Most opt for a gradual approach, starting slowly in the first trimester, peaking in the second, and plateauing in the third. But if she wants to gain sixty pounds in her first eight months, she's free to do so, so long as she spends the last month sweating off twenty-eight pounds at the track and/or the sauna.

As for what Mommy will look like a few years after you're born, those interested in an upbeat view are referred to the new DVD, *MILF Hunter 35: Gettin' Fre-K After Pre-K.*

A Fetal Examination®
CELEBRITY BABIES: ALMOST FETUS

A star is unborn!

First of all: great career move. Getting cast as "Adorable Hollywood Child" is going to open the door to dozens of better

opportunities, for to be born to—and then, to a tiny extent, raised by—celebrities is to be quite literally thrust into the spotlight.* News of your arrival will be heralded. People will come great lengths to catch a glimpse of you. Your image will be reprinted around the world. You'll feel just like Jesus, only the place *he* came out of isn't the subject of upskirts on celebritybeaver.org.

And it gets even better. No longer is a pregnant star obliged to "lie low." Nowadays, the masses

Fig. 26. *The 102,456,205,786th human couple to have children.*

want to hear how celebrities are "just like them," and evidence of a working reproductive system is a great way of feigning that kind

---

* Really. Hollywood delivery rooms are lit with spotlights. Plus they CGI the ultrasounds so it looks like you're gestating with an army of orcs.

of common humanity. There's even a special Hollywood name for the pregnancy belly. It's called a "baby bump"— "baby" as in "you," and "bump" as in "15 percent uptick in opening-weekend BO."*

There's only one small area where being a celebaby has a downside: **childhood**. You're going to experience a certain amount of emotional neglect. It's not that Mom and Dad won't share the same love and tenderness all new parents feel for their kids. It's just that rather than *feeling* it, you'll be *reading* about it. "Mommy has never been so fulfilled," you will discover in *Us Weekly*, and you will be happy for this "Mommy" person. As for those reports that compared with normal people, your parents are far more likely to suffer from alcoholism, drug abuse, and psychological problems . . . that may or may not be the case. What *is* certain is that *you* will suffer from these things, because depravity is to Hollywood what mosquitoes are to a bleeding naked man in a stagnant pool in a rainforest wearing a steak tartare hat. Luckily, your publicist will be there to minimize the fallout, and a small army of nannies, tutors, and other "parental stunt doubles" will tend to your nurturing and schooling needs, as long as you're willing to pass their screenplays on to your buddy at Paramount.

Two aspects of celebrabyhood deserve particular mention. The first is **nomenclature**. A star's last name is a ticket to fame and fortune. Realizing this, stars seek to ground their children by giving them *first* names that are tickets to noogies and wedgies. This tradition dates back to ancient Greece, when Alcibiades, the

> **UTERINE LINER NOTE**
>
> *"Awwww, yeah, that's right, motherfuckers! I'm goin' home with Meg Fuckin' Ryan! Have fun growing up with no parents in a country of 1.3 billion, 'cause guess what, douchebags? Zhao met Sally!"*
>
> ~~Hong Zhao~~
> Tobias Ryan
> ~~Shenghui Orphanage,~~
> ~~Shenghui, China~~
> Hollywood, CA

---

* Also, "bump" as in "inconvenient little nuisance that gets in the way."

most celebrated Athenian of his time, named his children Emily and Kevin. At the time, those were some stupid-ass names. But in christening a newborn Apple Martin, Kal-el Cage, Zowie Bowie, or Speck Wildhorse Mellencamp, today's celebrity does more than just tell him or her, "I love you enough to make cops mock your driver's license." It tells the world, "I'm so rich and famous I can get away with giving my child a name this fucking dumb."*

There is also the matter of **celebrity adoption**, the dream of every newborn African since the infant Moses floated his way to the big time. If you're not *born* to famous parents, don't give up hope. There is still a chance that you'll be spotted in your African orphanage by a visiting superstar. Should this opportunity arise, *look as big-eyed and hungry as humanly possible.* UN Goodwill Ambassadors don't pass through Gambia every day, and you'll be kicking yourself if you end up outcuted and it's little M'Chumb!waza next crib over who winds up a Clooney.

---

* Sadly, the new generation of celebrity parents does not respect the hierarchy. Woody Allen, David Bowie, and John Mellencamp are legends who *deserve* to misname their kids, but when some C-lister named Shannyn Sossamon names her child Audio Science, where's the respect? Come on, Shannyn. You haven't earned the right to call your kids anything weirder than Madisyn.

Celebraby Word Find

Find the first names of the sixteen celebrity children listed below in the grid (in any direction, vertically, horizontally, or diagonally). When you're done, the remaining letters, read left to right and top to bottom, will answer the question, "Why do famous people give their children such unusual names?"

```
L   T   N   A   E   C   O   H   E   Y   A   R
E   E   S   T   O   R   Y   J   C   O   L   J
V   U   R   M   A   P   L   E   N   T   L   E
U   A   O   E   N   L   Y   O   U   A   E   R
O   E   N   K   A   L   E   L   T   X   B   M
N   B   O   O   I   P   F   T   N   O   E   A
H   N   H   U   D   C   P   O   H   W   U   J
O   G   U   T   N   I   R   L   T   H   L   E
L   I   R   E   I   B   A   L   E   I   B   S
I   E   A   N   I   H   P   A   R   E   S   T
H   R   P   H   I   N   N   A   E   U   S   Y
S   L   E   G   N   A   E   U   L   B   T   Y
```

Apple (Chris Martin and Gwyneth Paltrow)

Banjo (Rachel Griffiths and some guy)

Blue Angel (The Edge and some chick)

Bluebell (Geri Halliwell and some guy)

Bronx (Ashlee Simpson and Pete Wentz)

Honor (Jessica Alba and Cash Warren)

Indiana (Casey Affleck and some chick)

Jermajesty (Jermaine Jackson and some chick)

Kal-el (Nicolas Cage and some chick)

Ocean (Forest Whitaker and some chick)

Phinnaeus (Julia Roberts and some guy)

Reignbeau (Ving Rhames and some chick)

Seraphina (Jennifer Garner and Ben Affleck)

Shiloh Nouvel (Angelina Jolie and Brad Pitt)

Story (Jenna Elfman and some guy)

Tu (Rob Morrow . . . get it?)

CHAPTER 6

Month 4

Pardon the Protrusion

For you, the start of Month 4 may feel like just another day at the office. But for Mom it marks the welcome beginning of the Goldilocks trimester: Neither too nauseous nor too bovine, she's feeling jusssssst right. Well, you'll show her. You'll show everybody. You'll **show**, period. It's high time you make your presence known to the world, so that everyone can see it's not that Mommy's been eating a lot lately . . . well, not *just* that.

Best Weeks Ever! 14–17

WEEK 14

You're really moving now—**flexing muscles**, **wiggling fingers**, and already demonstrating a broader range of motion than Richard Gere. Hungry? Consider snacking on one of the local delicacies: **your thumb**. It's quite flavorful, and it's not like you'll need it for hitchhiking anytime soon. By the way, *love* what you're doing with your **nails**—you know, having them—but we're not sure about the hair. Honestly, **lanugo**? A downy coat covering your whole body? We know it's just till you're born, but you did hear the Neanderthals died out, right?

WEEK 15

This is when it gets really hard to tell what fruit you're the same size as. Some say **apples**, others **tangerines**, but it's impossible to say for sure, as these vital comparisons have become yet another victim of the ongoing "turf war" between obstetricians and produce distributors. So we're just going to say **you're four inches long**. By the way, nice choice **moving your ears to the side of your head**. They look better there. The neck thing was . . . it was a little avant-garde.

WEEK 16

Well well well, look who's creating **urine**! Mazel tov on the excretory system. But word on the street is **you're peeing every forty-five minutes**. Slow down there, Tinkly—this a uterus, not a urethra! Okay, we can tell from the **small side-to-side movements of your eyes** that this is making you uncomfortable. Try not to be so thin-skinned. (Seriously, you're **translucent**. We can see all your blood vessels, for God's sake.)

WEEK 17

Listen, we need to talk. We care about you enough to tell you the truth. You've gotten **fat**. No, it's not much, but this is how it starts: a little today, a little tomorrow, and next thing you know, by the time you're born you're covered in baby fat, and who finds that attractive, especially with the childhood-obesity epidemic and everything? Anyway, just a little body-image issue to think about. Starting now. For the rest of your life.

What You May Be Concerned She's Not Concerned About

DISHONORABLE DISCHARGE

"I heard Mommy talking about some kind of milky white stuff coming out of her vagina. That's not, uh . . . that's not the same vagina I'm coming out of, is it?"

It is, but fear not. It's a substance called **leukorrhea**, after the province in Korrhea where it was first identified. Composed of secretions, old cells, bacteria, and half-and-half, it is usually odorless, though it sometimes comes in Pine Fresh. Mommy produced a little of it before you were conceived, but pregnancy increases the volume to the point where many women are forced to call a plumber. This discharge will climax a few weeks before birth with the dissolution of her **cervical mucous plug** (Fig. 27), when the leukorrhea thickens with the addition of blood-tinged, deep-dish mucus. "Don't go there!" you may

Fig. 27. *This image should help clear your mental palate after that mention of a* **cervical mucous plug**.

cry. But you *are* going there, and you'll be fine. So will Mommy. Chances are she'll just be buying a few more extra panty liners and a few less vanilla milk shakes.

WHO IS SHE WEARING (OTHER THAN YOU)?

"What color is Mom's parachute? Seriously, I'm curious. We're going out in public, and I'm assuming she's wearing a parachute."

Fig. 28. *All the rage in the '50s, the fiberglass sphere-gown catapulted its designer, Owens Corning, to the top of the fashion world.*

Are you kidding? Get with the times, boy- or girlfriend! **Pregnancy fashion** has come a long way since the days of the infamous "fiberglass sphere-gown" (Fig. 28). Today's woman can choose from a variety of stylish and comfortable looks that are at best form-fitting and at worst not form-mocking. More practically, many of these clothes will adjust as you and Mommy grow bigger, thanks to a well-hidden array of **straps, bands, buttons, bolts, hinges, clamps, clasps, hasps, knobs, levers, pulleys, ratchets, industrial-strength flanges,** and **steel-girded support beams.**

Of course, these clothes will only fit Mommy for a short time. To save money, she might want to consider **staying forty pounds overweight for the rest of her life.** Another, less stupid option is rummaging through her husband's drawers for T-shirts, running shorts, and sweatpants. It's a great way to find free, comfy clothes, and it's guaranteed to unearth a treasure trove of pornography. A third option is asking to borrow maternity clothes from friends. This she should do without guilt. She will loan them to someone else next year, just as someone loaned them to *her* friends *last* year. In fact, it's an open secret that the same 100,000

Fig. 29. *This maternity dress's lineage includes Patsy Cline, Chris Evert, Nancy Pelosi, and that guy who just had a baby.*

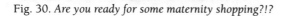

Fig. 30. *Are you ready for some maternity shopping?!?*

maternity dresses have been circulating around the world for the last half-century (Fig. 29).

But such "sloppy seconds" are no match for the exciting new fashions awaiting Mommy at her local mall. And when she goes hunting for those fashions, she'd be wise to bring along her chief fashion consultant and shopping companion—**Daddy**. Like all men, he is tremendously interested in the nuances of maternity fashion, so there's nothing he'd rather be doing than accompanying his beloved as she tries on every single garment in the store. Particularly on Sunday afternoons in the fall (Fig. 30).

OPINIONS ARE LIKE AND/OR OFFERED BY ASSHOLES

"Mom doesn't know how to deal with all the unsolicited advice she's getting. What advice can you offer her unsolicitedly?"

Pregnancy brings out the Nosey Nellie in everyone. When Mom orders a coffee at Starbucks, some barista is sure to say, "A latte?

Relax!

The pressure of developing a body getting to you? Here's a helpful meditation exercise to calm even the most anxious fetus. Imagine yourself lying serenely on soft blankets in a warm room, your every need attended to by two loving yet obedient servants. Then, working your way up from toes to face, concentrate on growing each and every part of you to maximize the cuteness those servants worship. If you practice this routine every day, you'll be able to sustain this perfect lifestyle for twelve to eighteen months!

That's not a good idea." At dinner, the patron at the next table may sneer, "A Caesar salad? *That's* not a wise choice." Even in bed, the man next to her may muse, "No blow job? *That's* not healthy for the baby."

It would be hard enough for Mommy to deal with such meddlesome people if their advice was wrong. But it's not. It's right. The barista, the patron, the man in the bed—they were correct. Her sister's loud harangue at the Thanksgiving table, her co-worker's whispered aside at the watercooler, even the doorman's disapproving stare when she got home last night—all were based on real and obvious failures in your mother's pregnancy skills, failures everyone she meets gets together to talk about when she's not around.

Our advice on *their* advice? When a stranger offers a "helpful suggestion," Mommy should politely but firmly tell him she's doing just fine on her own,

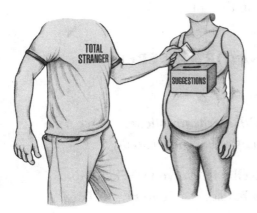

Fig. 31.

Ask an Old Wife

Q: Where do you get your tales, anyway?

A: What kind of impertinent query is
that, young lady? My tales descend di-
rectly from my ancestors, thirteen generations of the most elderly, most married
women in all of New England, who
passed their knowledge down through

the centuries uncontaminated by science and free from the corruption
of reason. So when I say an unborn's gender can be divined by which
side a holly leaf falls on when dropped upon a damask bush at dusk, I
speak with the authority inherited from my great-great-great-great-
great-great-grandmother Temperance, who as Elderwoman of Salem
formulated the "witches swim, innocent sink" hypothesis!

Thanks for thy question!

thank you very much. Then, as soon as the person's gone, she
should *immediately* put his suggestion into practice. This compromise will allow her to save face and maintain her dignity
while still letting the stranger's advice help pick up the slack for
her staggering incompetence.

As for those (not infrequent) cases when Mommy is given
two diametrically opposed directives, she should simply find a
way to implement both through a Zen-like breakthrough to a
higher plane of reality.

Around the World in Forty Weeks

America isn't the only nation where people get pregnant. In fact, the natives of more than forty-five countries reproduce in the exact same way. A sample of some international pregnancy-related factoids:

Australia	Unborn babies = "bludgeroos"; pregnant women = "tammywobbles"
Brazil	Mandatory second-trimester screening for ass size
China	Apgar test consisting of balance beam and floor exercises
Cuba	New fathers, mothers, *and* babies smoke cigars
France	Slang term for pregnancy: *"une baguette dans la terrine"*
India	Prenatal care synced with terminal-patient care for smoother karmic transition
Israel	Fetuses continually hounded by mothers for "never calling"
Mexico	Water broken by blindfolded child with stick
Namibia	All ultrasounds FedExed to Brangelina

THE SISTERHOOD OF THE TRAVELING STRETCH PANTS

"My parents are thinking about going on vacation. What the hell?! I don't get to lie on the beach in Barbados for a week!"

Well, you kind of do, actually. And you might want to show a little compassion. Remember: This is Mom and Dad's last chance to go on vacation for *twelve years*. They owe it to themselves to check in to a resort and spend one week doing little more than eating,

Panama	Birth canals exceptionally long, owned by government
Peru	Machu Picchu General Hospital renowned for quality of care, breathtaking inconvenience
Russia	"Vodka births" increasingly common
Saudi Arabia	Girls in womb forbidden from "kicking suggestively"
Sweden	IKEA-made intrauterine furniture provides affordable comfort
Switzerland	Due date includes hour, minute, and second
Vatican City	New pregnancies greeted with mix of shock and covert pride

swimming, and just lying there . . . the kind of existence *some* lucky bastards get to enjoy every single day.

A word about airline travel: Many airlines have strict rules about allowing pregnant women on planes.* These rules usually concern the point in the pregnancy after which she will not be

UTERINE LINER NOTE

"I went with my parents on their trip to Paris. What a thrill it was to hear the Eiffel Tower."

—Week 27, Oak Park, Illinois

* The rules for *impregnating* women on planes are even stricter.

allowed to board, and range from Week 32 (American Airlines) to the baby's head sticking out (Delta). Otherwise, as long as she takes it easy, stays hydrated, and adopts a laissez-faire attitude toward peeing in the pool, there's nothing wrong with Mommy kicking back on a deck chair, sipping a virgin colada, and soaking in the sun one last time in that sexy red-and-black two-piece that will never truly fit her again.

A Fetal Examination®
EXERCISE AND FETALCY:
NINE MONTHS TO A NEW YOU!

What kind of exercise program is right for you and Mommy? That's a two-part question.

Let's start with Mom. For most of history, mothers were expected to follow a strict regimen of bed rest. The Victorians euphemized pregnancy as "feeling delicate" and expected women to "lie in" in a "state of confinement" until it was time to "colonize their Punjab." But the days of doing nothing all day but reading and sleeping and having friends over and being pampered by a team of servants are, thankfully, over. We now know that a regular workout routine does wonders for a pregnant woman's physical, mental, and emotional health and, when done at a crowded gym, can shame twenty paunchy men into two hundred ab crunches in less than a minute.

Of course, certain exercises make more sense than others. Swimming is a good activity; scuba diving is not. A StairMaster is a safe choice; a StairFaller, less so. Thirty minutes on a rowing machine? Excellent. Thirty minutes in an X-ray machine? Even better!

A growing number of gyms offer classes featuring exercises

Weeble-Wobble

▲ Kneel on floor in four-point stance. Lift all four limbs into air. Weeble; wobble. Do not fall down.

Downward-Facing Pregnant Dog

▲ Assume classic yoga position. Inhale. Hold for twenty seconds. Exhale. Raise self with forklift.

Judon't

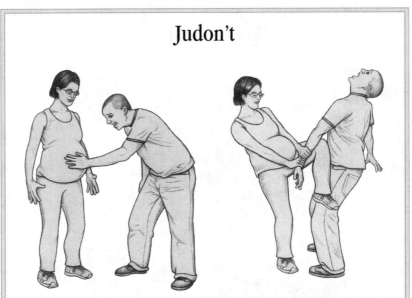

▲ Stand with feet shoulder width apart on the middle of the sidewalk. Wait for total stranger to place hand on stomach without asking. Kick leg up in circular motion, dislocating stranger's elbow.

Memory Drill

▲ Stand in profile against a mirror. Flexing "core" muscles, attempt to reshape silhouette to resemble old self. Repeat until sad.

designed exclusively for pregnant women (see illustrations). But whatever her workout, Mom should be careful to ease her way into it. Before hitting the treadmill at the gym, for example, she should stretch, jog slowly for a few minutes, rest, order a smoothie, get dressed, and leave the gym.

There's one exercise you will feel Mommy doing all the time, and its story is a heroic one. Since the dawn of history, mankind has labored in pursuit of a common goal: the strengthening of the pubococcygeus muscles of a woman's pelvis. Many a brave gynecologist embarked on this noble quest, each seeking immortality, each falling short. Yet the dream never died, and in 1948, Dr. Arnold H. Kegel finally made it a reality with his invention of **Kegel exercises**. Dr. Kegel is gone now, yet he lives on. Wherever vulvas need tightening, Kegel is there. Wherever bladders need regulating, Kegel is there. Wherever postpartum women contract their anal canals around vaginal barbells, Kegel is there.

Kegel exercises help ease the pain caused by squeezing an entire human being out of a place that used to only fit a very small part of one. Which brings us to the second half of the exercise equation: **you**. Given your busy schedule and the relative lack of Nautilus equipment, it's tempting to spend what little free time you have just curled up in a ball watching the tube. Don't. This is *precisely* the time to start developing workout habits that will last the rest of your life before birth. The following are a few suggestions that will hopefully set you down the path to fetal fitness. Now, get out there and (after developing sweat glands) sweat!

Somersault

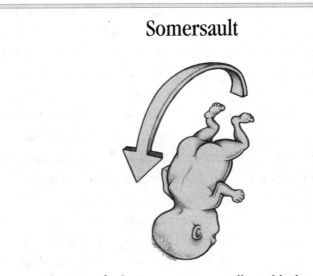

▲ A good exercise for beginners. Using small, steplike leg motions, rotate entire body 360 degrees along transverse axis. More advanced: backward somersault. Most advanced: armstand backward one-and-a-half-somersault tuck with half-twist.

Toe Curls

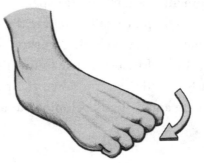

▲ While inhaling, slowly curl the itsy-bitsy cutie-wootie wizzu toesie-woesies on your left foot. Exhale and uncurl. Repeat ten times. Turn and repeat with itsy-bitsy cutie-wootie wizzu toesie-woesies on right foot.

Limb Thrash

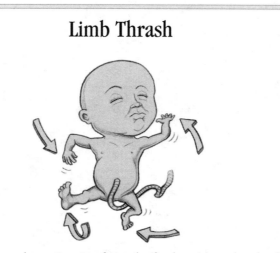

▲ A rigorous workout. Starting from the fetal position, thrash all four limbs wildly about as if you just noticed them and are trying to figure out exactly what they do. Very dehydrating—be sure to suck plenty of thumb.

Boxing

▲ "The sweet science" has become an increasingly popular aerobic exercise during the third trimester, for boys *and* girls. Current pennyweight division champion: No Name "The Week 28 Walloper" Kaminski.

CHAPTER 7

Month 5

Acknowledging Your Flailings

Y ou have reached the halfway point of your extraordinary journey from nonexistence to total helplessness. You're ready to take the first step toward transforming your *dependent* relationship with Mommy into the *codependent* one you'll have after Daddy leaves. This is done by punching, kicking, careening, and generally acting like a drunk Mel Gibson until Mommy finally realizes, "That's not the chimichanga . . . *it's the baby!*" It's a wondrous process called **quickening**, after the popular software program many mothers use to keep track of it.

Best Weeks Ever! 18–22

WEEK 18

So you've started **yawning**. Good! We were wondering when you'd notice just how boring womb life really is. You've also begun **hiccupping**. Weird, ain't it? Feels like you're dry-heaving a metronome. It can be cured by a sudden shock, so remember: **You will soon be emerging from your mother's post-leukorrheic vagina.**

WEEK 19

What's white, cheesy, and reminds you of grease? If you said John Travolta, partial credit! But the real answer is **vernix caseosa**, the stuff now covering your skin. (Trivia: Vernix caseosa is also the real name of actor/director Vincent Gallo!) It keeps you from wrinkling. Without it, you'd come out looking like Madonna's elbows.

WEEK 20

Let's talk about **sex**. Like, yours. 'Cause you have one, and right about now is when your parents can find out what it is. But that's *their* concern. More to the point, do *you* want to know? A lot of fetuses choose not to "look down" until birth, preferring to be surprised. Others choose to learn right away so they can get a jump start on wanting to be either an astronaut or a princess. To peek or not to peek? It's entirely your decision. Just like being gay.

WEEK 21

Officially halfway home! Why not celebrate with a few shots of **amniotic fluid**? It's a thirst quencher, and it'll improve your **swallowing** and **digesting**, skills many people who eat food find useful. Make a party of it. Drink, dance, kick, twist, turn, somersault—get out there and rage against the Ma scene! Then, pass out at your place. And don't worry about setting the alarm: You should be getting twelve to fourteen hours of **sleep** a day at this point, so feel free to snooze until noon, then open wide and drink up some hair of the amniotic dog!

Latin: Dead Language of the Unborn

Whether it's euphemizing something gross or just sounding smart in front of patients, Latin is the go-to language for all things awkward and obstetric. Can you match the definitions on the left with the words on the right?

Yellow circle in archery : nipple :: Red circle in archery : _____	**Candida albicans**
Vaginal inflammation caused by parasitic yeastlike fungus with lilting name	**leukorrhea**
Birthmarks . . . only it's your birth but her marks	**chloasma**
The amuse-bouche of breast-feeding	**lochia**
If you're born looking like Albino Bigfoot, blame this	**areola**
What's going down? Not Daddy, if Mommy has this	**perineum**
Looks like Mommy's navel leaked cappuccino	**lanugo**
Postnatal drip	**colostrum**
By two days after birth, you'll be too old for this shit	**linea nigra**
Snobby-ass word for "taint"	**meconium**
Cheesy; superficial; associated with birth; not this book	**vernix caseosa**

Answers (from top to bottom): areola, Candida albicans, chloasma, colostrum, lanugo, leukorrhea, linea nigra, lochia, meconium, perineum, vernix caseosa

KICKING MOM OLD SCHOOL

"I'm at Week 19, and I'm kicking as hard as I can, but I heard Mom say it 'tickles, like butterflies fluttering.' Am I doing something wrong?"

(Author's note: This question will be guest-answered by one of the world's leading authorities on this subject, Mr. Kesuke Miyagi.)

Hai!

You have much to learn, fetus-san. What, you think you kick and elbow, it get Mom pay attention? Is not the way.

Karate not for to worry Mom, little bonsai. Karate for not *have* to worry Mom. Stop kicking and punching, *then* she get worried. Eat entire bag mini Kit Kats just get you smack her inside.

Mom, she also have wrong idea. Place Dad's hand on belly for to feel. Think it make him one

WEEK 22

Kudos! In a mere six months, you've grown to a pound. In thirty years, it'll take you that long just to *lose* one. You probably have **hair**, though right now it's bright white. (Talk about premature gray!) You also have **eyelashes** and **eyebrows**; if you have a **unibrow**, consider yourself stigmatized for life. Your **eyesight**'s im-

with fetus-san. No understand: Dad feel kick, mind go right to scene in *Alien* where dragon-creature pop out man's stomach.

So. You want become master of uterine kicking? Then must train. Study prenatal martial arts. Go by many names: *Tyke won do, ai kiddo, yung fu.* Ready begin? Must ask no questions. Trust Miyagi. Your womb my dojo.

You see walls all around you? You must whack them with foot. Then sleep. Then whack them with elbow. Then sleep. Whack, sleep, whack, sleep. Whacks on, whacks off. Whacks on, whacks off. Left, right. Up, down. Side, side. Breathe in, breathe out. And no break sac or big trouble.

Fig. 32. *No care how many Oscars she win. She always Next Karate Kid to Miyagi.*

Hai! You promise no ask questions! "What color belt I wear?" I no wear belt. You know who else no wear belt? Your mom. She big as sumo.

Now go practice and no complain. I back soon. Must go hospital. Try to deliver baby with chopstick. Man who deliver baby with chopstick can accomplish anything.

proving, and you've got a **firm grip** that you're likely using to tug on the umbilicus. That's cool, but bear in mind that cord is not an emergency brake. Like it or not, in eighteen weeks, this train is pulling into the station.

What You May Be Concerned She's Not Concerned About

Fig. 33. *The unborn Mozart was the only fetus in history to compose music in the womb to stimulate his mother's intellectual development.*

EINE KLEINE ANNOYING MUSIK

"Can you tell me why my parents blast Mozart at me every night right when I'm trying to fucking sleep?!"

This is a weird one.

Your parents want the best for you. They want you to be better than themselves and not to suffer from the same failings they believe they have. And one of these failings is that they never, ever, ever listen to classical music. It's not that they necessarily hate it. Some of it, they may even think, is not so bad. But it bores them, and they simply don't have the time to sit back and learn to appreciate it. You, on the other hand, *do*. So to assuage their guilt, you get an involuntary nine-month subscription to your very own Mostly Mozart Festival . . . in a room with very bad acoustics.*

For Mom and Dad, you represent unmolded clay, an empty canvas, a *tabula rasa* (Arabic for chickpea salad with rice and parsley). By filling your womb with Mozart or Bach, they hope to expedite your intellectual development. They envision you reading by age one, speaking three languages by age six, graduating from MIT by age twelve, and making your first friend by age thirty-eight.

* Those sporadic loud *splat* sounds? Let's just say they ain't coming from no magic flute.

Fig. 34. *Named for and activated by the protrusion of Mommy's navel, the iPop can hold up to 400 hours of music or 3,000 ultrasounds.*

It's a concept that—*in theory*—sounds stupid. And research has indeed found that prenatal music education has little effect. In one study, twenty-five third-trimester women were exposed to Tchaikovsky's *1812 Overture* around the clock for a week. A year later, only three of the babies had successfully defended Russia

The Alternative Scene

If Mommy is willing to experiment, she'll discover music far hipper than stodgy old Mozart—and far more appropriate for the fetal environment. Some suggestions:

"Be My Baby," The Ronettes

"I'm Coming Out," Diana Ross

"Kid Inside," John Mellencamp

"I've Got You Under My Skin," Frank Sinatra

"Keep On Growing," Eric Clapton

"Alive and Kicking," Simple Minds

"In My Room," The Beach Boys

"Should I Stay or Should I Go?" The Clash

"The Waiting," Tom Petty and the Heartbreakers

"With or Without You," U2 (conjoined twins only)

UTERINE LINER NOTE

"The first time I heard Mozart in my womb, I cursed God for bestowing such genius on such a rogue. Revenge, I swore! Revenge!!!"

—Antonio Salieri,
eight months old, Vienna

from Napoleon's armies. And there are some definite downsides associated with the philharmonicization of your uterus. Not only does it disrupt your sleep, but given the contemporary associations of classical music, hearing it may make you feel like you're being "put on hold," a fetus forced to wait eternally for a maternal-service technician who never picks up.

What *is* true is that your sense of hearing is now developed enough to absorb sounds, and the most important of these by far are the voices of your mommy and daddy. (The former will come in Dolby®-quality surround sound, the latter in Jolson-era mono.) They're the voices of two people who love you, and as such you may very well find them stimulating and soothing, assuming you're not the love child of Fran Drescher and Henry Kissinger.

As for the music, try to let it fade into the background. It could have been a whole lot worse. At least it's Mozart—not Boulez!!!

EINE KLEINE FOLLOW-UP

"Who's Boulez?"

Oh, sorry. He's a twentieth-century French composer who writes in a radical post-Webernian serialist idiom many find jarring. That was the basis of the joke. We thought . . . we'd assumed you were culturally aware enough to . . . never mind. Mozart is pretty.

NEXT OF SKIN

"The other day I heard Mommy complain I'm making her body look like a Jackson Pollock painting. What does she mean?"

She's referring to the various abstract expressionistic flourishes on display on her **skin** right now.*

Some soon-to-be mothers expect to bask in "the glow of pregnancy," a physical and spiritual radiance emanating from the core of their being. Presumably, this glow is created in Santa's workshop before being handed off to the Easter Bunny, who swims to Neverland, where Tinker Bell picks it up and carries it in a butterfly-wing suitcase straight to her pet unicorn. It's actually far more common for Mommy to experience dermatological *problems* during pregnancy, due to the hormones pulsing through her, penetrating her skin's melanin cells and switching their chemical settings from "docile" to "impish."

Of all pregnancy's side effects, skin changes are by definition the most superficial, and thus the worst. They include:

Fig. 35. *Born José Antonio Domínguez, Banderas adopted his mother's surname as his stage name. The rest is history!*

- **The mask of pregnancy (chloasma).** This blotchy facial discoloration appears dark on light-skinned women, light on dark-skinned women, and zigzag on plaid-skinned women. It is not to be confused with *The Mask of Zorro,* the searing 1998 epic drama starring the smoldering Antonio Banderas (Fig. 35)!

- **Hyperpigmentation.** Freckles, moles, nipples, and areolas grow darker. In extreme cases they can only be seen in ultraviolet light.

---

* Although a better analogy would have been Rothko. She said Pollock?! Christ. Now we know where you got "Who's Boulez?" from.

Mommy's Skin Being "Rash"?

Maybe if she'd bought a copy of *What® to Expect When You're® Expected: Health and Beauty Edition* like we'd asked her to, she wouldn't look like such a freak.

Fig. 36. *At least the black line isn't her fault.*

- **Linea nigra.** The usually invisible white line running down the center of Mommy's abdomen turns black, providing a helpful arrow to the place you will soon need to travel to (Fig. 36).
- **Stretch marks.** Also known as "ten pounds of shit in a five-pound bag" syndrome.

Many of these problems are compounded by exposure to the sun, so Mommy should wear sunblock outdoors and, if possible, avoid prolonged open-ocean survival ordeals.

THE VELVET ULTRASOUND

"My parents know I'm healthy. Why do they keep taking pictures of me?"

Because they're crazy about **recreational ultrasound**, the superfluous invasive procedure craze that's sweeping the nation!

For too long, moms and dads had to wait until birth to see what their child looked like. You can see the problem: By the time you're born, you're cute. Do parents really want their first impression of you to be "Aw, isn't he adorable?" Of course not! They want it to be "Eww, isn't he creepy and alien-looking?"

That's where recreational ultrasound comes in. It's offered at boutique franchises across the country, often in malls, where they thrive in a tucked-between-Foot-Locker-and-Johnny-Rockets milieu that inspires total confidence. For a few hundred dollars, certified medical-style Nursettes® will take high-quality 3- and 4-D pictures of you. They'll even leave the ultrasound on for minutes at a time, so Mom and Dad can see your every kick, breath, and embarrassed squirm. When they leave, they'll take with them a DVD and an unforgettable series of coppery images that look like someone engraved your face on a penny, then baked it.

To be sure, there are critics. Some consider recreational ultrasound a "gateway" to other, harder procedures. Others note that the history of medicine is filled with allegedly "safe" practices that were later found harmful, such as bloodletting and lava enemas. A handful quibble that common sense dictates you don't subject a fetus to five minutes of intense ultrasonic energy just for the sake of having a disturbing blurry snapshot to shove in the face of the woman trapped next to you on the plane. A few pesky curmudgeons even wonder what the hell the rush is that you can't wait to see your kid at the time and place nature fucking intended.

But for many, the weekly ultrasound has become as much a part of an all-American pregnancy routine as Tequila Tuesdays and failing to quit smoking. So if you find yourself posing for the umpteenth time this trimester, don't fret—just smile and say "It's not advisable for pregnant women to eat soft cheeeeeeeeeese!"

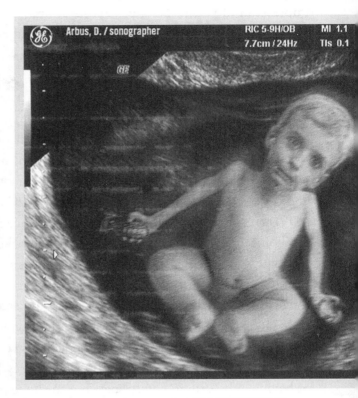

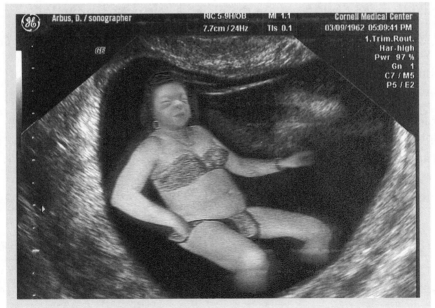

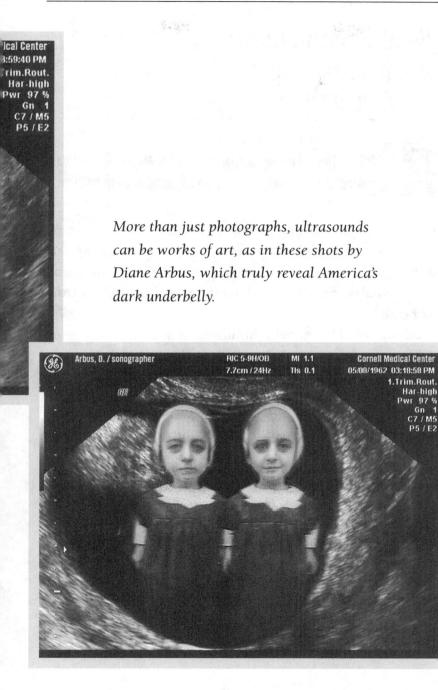

More than just photographs, ultrasounds can be works of art, as in these shots by Diane Arbus, which truly reveal America's dark underbelly.

A Fetal Examination®
SEX DURING PREGNANCY:
THREAT OR BETRAYAL?

 NOTE: The following section is rated R for graphic sexual content. No one under 17 may be admitted outside a parent.

Mom's already pregnant with you, so why does Daddy keep re-inseminating her? Don't get paranoid—they're not having second thoughts about you. They're just engaging in the innocent, perfectly wholesome act of **rubbing their genitals inches from your head**.

Nothing could be more beautiful, right? Yet for some reason, many parents have been led to believe that **sex during pregnancy is wrong**. This false assertion is based on a series of myths: that **the unborn fetus is watching Daddy's penis move inside Mommy's vagina**; that *the penis comes in direct contact with the placenta during intercourse*; even that *THE FORCE OF MOMMY'S ORGASM WILL MAKE THE BABY CONVULSE IN DISGUST*. What a shame their minds are filled with images like these, rather than joyous ones, like that of themselves and their unborn baby happily sharing a ménage à trois.*

> **UTERINE LINER NOTE**
>
> *"My parents had sex many times while I was in the womb, and it didn't do me any damage at all. Now, where's my teddy bear? I want to fuck it."*
>
> —Jennifer G., six months old, Cherry Hill, New Jersey

First things first: From a health standpoint, intercourse is extremely safe during low-risk pregnancies, and extremely fun dur-

---

* Next time your Daddy worries he's hurting you, he should take a moment to think about the amniotic fluid, the strong uterine muscles, and the mucus plug blocking the cervix. That should get him thrusting again.

Look Out, Coprophilia!

Maieusophoria—the eroticization of pregnancy—is one of America's fastest-growing sexual fetishes. Its aficionados are aroused by fantasies of protruding bellies, lactation, and birth-control pills being flushed down the toilet. This carnal passion for pregnant women is shared by an estimated two million Americans, an estimated none of whom are married to Mommy.

ing high-risk marriages. In certain instances, a doctor may advise a woman to abstain from sex, but it's more common for him to simply advise her not to reach orgasm. Nine times out of ten, this has no impact whatsoever on sex with her husband.

But pregnancy's effect on your parents' libido is, unlike your umbilical cord, rarely cut-and-dried. Some women's physical woes all but erode their sex drive, and their daily refrain becomes "Not tonight, I have a fetus." Others find the combination of hormones, increased pelvic blood flow, and their newly Mullally-esque figure arousing; they feel like fertility goddesses and want their partners to serve as Earth Motherfuckers. But the partner may meet the woman's "come hither" leer with a "go thither" glare, and not just because of her new shape. Remember, until a few months ago he'd truly believed the sole purpose of his wife's sexual organs was to give him something to do after *CSI*.

Given all this, it's no wonder many couples opt for other ways to satisfy their need for intimacy during this time, such as kissing, sighing, pouting, sulking, and looking at each other in tacit recognition that an era has passed. But for those who do take the plunge, sex during pregnancy can be a wonderfully joyous experience in which two souls standing at the threshold of parenthood unite in a transcendent blah blah blah, yada yada.

Here's the truth: Pregnancy transforms sex from a spontaneous expression of love and desire to a prolonged exercise in not hurting each other. That's why the favorite sexual position for many soon-to-be mommies and daddies is "no." Other, less passive-aggressive ones include:

- **Woman on top.** Daddy lies down on bed as Mommy straddles him. Caution: By end of term, may lead to comically Daddy-shaped indentation on mattress.
- **Edge of the bed.** Mommy lies on edge of bed; Daddy stands. Not recommended for top bunks.
- **Sitting.** Daddy sits in sturdy chair, legs spread, hips tipped up forty-five degrees. Mommy hands him remote. He masturbates to porn.
- **Sideways.** Mommy and Daddy lie on sides facing each other. Intimate, loving, tender. Estimated ejaculation time: six to eight weeks.
- **Reentry.** By far the most comfortable position. Daddy mounts Mommy as they float in zero gravity on rocket reentering Earth's atmosphere.
- **Spooning.** Mommy lies on left side; Daddy lies on side behind her. They both eat soup.
- **The usual.** Mommy lies on side, tilted back, with pillow wedged under back for support. Daddy attends business meeting in Chicago and will be home Friday.

And a few final alternatives:

- **Anal sex.** Just fine, and, depending on how *you* come out, maybe something they should have been doing more of.
- **Oral sex.** One caveat: Mom can get an embolism if Daddy blows into her vagina. There goes his patented "Dizzy Gillespie" move.
- **Vibrators and dildos.** Hey, they're sticking twenty kinds of machines up there for *your* sake—can't *she* stick *one* up there for *hers*?

CHAPTER 8

Month 6

Threshold of Unabortability

S tarting to feel real, isn't it? You've come a long way, not-yet-baby. But don't start packing your placenta just yet. There are still four months to go—although you wouldn't know it from those periodic squeezing sensations you're feeling. They're called **Braxton Hicks contractions**, and consider them the first of millions of mixed messages Mommy will be sending throughout your life. Still, you might want to take it easy on her. Not to say she's hormonal, but she just spent twenty minutes sobbing because Joanie just went on her first real date with the Fonz's nephew.

Best Weeks Ever! 23–27

WEEK 23

Look at you, with that happy pinkish glow! Is it love? Or just the **capillaries and veins now visible under your skin**? Whatever it is, it's doing wonders for your complexion. You go, girl/boy! Also, you've got a **pancreas**. Not sure what that's for, actually. Something to do with lymph, maybe? Dunno. Anyhoo, we're just glad you've finally decided to **unplug your nostrils**. That's going to make it a whole lot easier for you to—hey, get your finger out of there!

WEEK 24

Here's why we're so excited: Up till now, you didn't really have a *look,* you know? But now **your face is almost fully formed**, and you . . . are . . . *beautiful!* See? We told you to coalesce your features more anthropically! We're breathing a lot easier—and so are you, now that you've started **breathing**.

WEEK 25

Your **vocal cords** are working, but don't bother talking—with all the, shall we say, "ambient noise" in the vicinity, no one's gonna hear a word. Your **bones** are beginning to harden, as is Mommy's attitude toward the name Marissa. (She thinks it's pretentious.) Time to really start focusing on that **brain** of yours. All that **sensory information** you've been stockpiling? Why not try processing it? You'll be amazed at how much you learn!

WEEK 26

Another week, another new experiential modality. This time, it's **sight**. Yes, you're seeing things, and no, you're not crazy. View-wise, of course, it's not the Grand Canyon; more like Mammoth Caves. But the paparazzi (and mamarazzi) are on to you now. At a candid moment they're likely to crowd around right next to you and shine a flashlight in your face. It's like they're *trying* to get a rise out of you! Well, don't sink to their level. If you respond with kicking or some other type of violence, you're no better than them.

WEEK 27

Let's see, let's see . . . looking at your calendar here . . . buh buh buh . . . doesn't appear to be much on your schedule this week . . . your Tuesday 9:00 canceled . . . yeah, you're pretty clear till Friday. Oh, you do have a **flexure of the neural tube to form three cerebral vesicles** penciled in for 2:30. Honestly? You don't want to cancel that one.

What You May Be Concerned She's Not Concerned About

WHERE THE RUBBER MEETS THE LOAD

"Mommy lets strangers rub me ten times a day! What kind of sicko is she?"

Don't blame her; she's none too thrilled with it either. But a pregnant woman's belly is public property that may be touched, poked, and prodded by any U.S. citizen. It's an age-old custom that became the law of the land in 2003, when George W. Bush, in the most Orwellian act of his entire presidency, signed the No Child Left Unrubbed Act (Fig. 37).

Fig. 37. *"Oh, what an adorable human hand! May I feel it against Mom's gravid abdomen? Wow, I can even feel the pinky!"*

The longer a pregnancy wears on, the more the beautiful thing inside Mommy brings out the perverted *frotteur* inside everybody else. Why? Bewilderment. People just can't figure out how one person made his or her way inside *another* person. The geometry just doesn't seem right. It's like a ship in a bottle. No *way* that could have gotten in there. In this case, even seeing isn't believing; so, to confirm that the mammalian reproductive system continues to operate as it has for the last 100 million years, it becomes necessary to feel Mommy up in the supermarket.

As noted, there's nothing she can legally do about it. But there are ways she can discourage unwanted contact. Perhaps the most effective is to simply **touch back**. If a stranger reaches for her belly, she can reach for his. If he begins *rubbing* her belly, she can *rub* his. If his hand moves down to her genitals, she should do likewise. Many a fine third-trimester romance has blossomed in this way. She might also consider a little white lie, like "I have a stomach rash," or a little "white truth," like "The thought of your fat hands touching my midriff makes me want to mouth-shit." But the majority of women choose to take it in stride. Some learn to enjoy it. A handful paint RUB ME on their stomachs, then work the reception line at weddings in a tank top. They are very, very needy.

BIGFOOT SIGHTING!

"I notice Mommy has begun wearing 'sensible shoes.' Is there, umm, something about her I should know?"

You mean, is she a lesbian? Only her motorcycle repairwoman knows for sure! But it *is* likely that she's suffering from **edema**, a swelling of the lower extremities typical of both Hillary Clinton and pregnancy. It's caused by the excess fluid she's retaining, which gravitates downward, turning ankles into cankles and cankles into shcankles.*

Edema is one of pregnancy's most common maladies. It's why

---

* Ankle + calf + shin.

Another Good Book

The Bible is the *What® to Expect When You're® Expected* of religious testaments.

---

she's wearing those shoes, and why she's spending so much time lying down, or with her feet propped up, or suspended upside down on a trapeze. It's why she just bought that pair of Hanes Pale Gray UltraScratchy Acute Support® pantyhose—the kind with compression knitting and a lead gusset. And it's why she's eating so many of the remarkable anti-swelling Japanese soybeans known as **edemame**.

Mommy's best remedy for those swollen feet? Hydrating *more*. Believe it or not, the more water she consumes, the more water she'll flush out. (Note: A similar strategy does *not* work for constipation.)

TUSKS

"What's with Mommy's tusks?"

Another of pregnancy's frequent side effects, **tusks** appear on approximately 50 percent of expectant women (Fig. 38). Breaking the skin near the end of the second trimester, they grow slowly, attaining a length of fifteen to eighteen inches (around the size of a walrus's) by full term. They may curve in slightly like a walrus's or bend upward

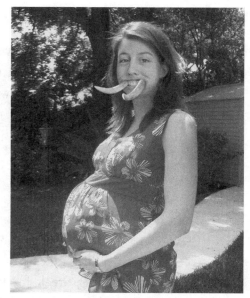

Fig. 38. *A majestically tusked pregnant woman.*

Make Pregnancy Last Forever!

A time capsule is a fun way for Mom and Dad to gather memories of this period in their lives. They can just stop by their local time capsulery, then fill their purchase with mementoes from "life before baby": photos, newspapers, alarm clocks, unstained clothing, stubs of movies they were able to see, matchbooks from restaurants they were able to eat at, postcards from countries they were able to vacation in, and a clay molding of Mom's firm, high, supple breasts. No need to bury it—they can simply cremate it in a somber ceremony.

like an elephant's. They weaken, shrivel, and fall off naturally a few weeks after birth. Sadly, most contemporary women conceal their tusks due to the ever-present threat of poaching.

THE FISSURE QUEEN

"Poor Mom's suffering from rectal bleeding."

And no doubt she's finding it very worrisome. But the good news is **recital bleeding** is a threat to neither you nor her, though it certainly can make for an awkward recital. There are several ways to—

UMMM . . .

"Excuse me, I didn't say—"

—ways to deal with the problem, depending on when in the recital the bleeding takes place. If it occurs in the middle of a movement, a long break in the music will be required, as the piano will need to be washed. However, if—

UMMM . . .

"I think you misunderstood me—"

—if the bleeding takes place between pieces, the performer may be able to apply a Band-Aid or tourniquet before blood drips on the keys, and the recital can continue with little or no delay. So there's your answer.

UMMM . . .

"I was actually asking about—"

We know what you were asking about, and it's disgusting. Let's move on.

A Fetal Examination®
CHILDBIRTH EDUCATION: READIN', WRITIN', AND RHYTHMIC BREATHIN'

As the big day nears, it's natural to start getting a little scared about your delivery, especially if you've never been born before. Well, you're not alone. Mommy, too, is beginning to fret. If you're her first child, she's probably dreading the pain that comes with labor. If you're not her first child, she's *absolutely* dreading it.

Until 150 years ago, new mothers were almost completely ignorant about the ordeal they were in for. All they knew was that it hurt like hell, frequently led to death, and for some reason seemed to require the continuous fetching of large amounts of hot water in old-timey pails. The picture changed with the invention of anesthesia. Now a mommy could spend most of your childbirth unconscious on her bed. After that, Daddy could spend most of your child*hood* unconscious on his.

But in the last thirty years, a new field has been born: **childbirth education**.* The proliferation of so many different classes, techniques, approaches, and philosophies means women no longer enter the delivery room ignorant and scared. They enter it overwhelmed and terrified. It's a huge step forward. It's also gotten Daddy much more involved, which benefits everybody, with the possible exception of Daddy.

As mentioned, there are many kinds of childbirth classes, but all share similar goals:

- To impart accurate, fair information about how their particular method of childbirth is awesome and how all other methods suck ass.
- To familiarize parents with various nightmare scenarios that might otherwise not have occurred to them.
- To empower Mommy with a personalized birthing plan that she will inevitably abandon immediately upon admission to the hospital.
- To teach real-world methods of breathing, distraction, and relaxation that will help Daddy get through the class.
- To introduce parents to other couples whose physical appearance and interpersonal dynamics will provide fodder for endless hours of bitchy conversation.

These are the laudable aims of all childbirth-education classes. Yet the ways in which these aims are pursued vary

---

* Ironically, the birth of childbirth education itself took several years and was very painful.

widely. Some approaches are more interactive. Some focus on co-ordination between couples. Some grade on a curve. Some are open only to high school seniors who've scored a 4 or 5 on their AP Childbirth test.

In choosing a class, there are several factors to consider:

- **Sponsorship.** Under whose guidance is the program being run? A doctor? The International Longshoremen's Association? A doula? If it's the last one, there could be problems.
- **Size.** A tip: Avoid any birthing class whose registration is handled by Ticketmaster.
- **Curriculum.** What are the lectures? What are the books? Do they make you read Henry James? If so, is it *Washington Square,* or one of his later novels that are impossible to wade through?*
- **Format.** Are films of real childbirths shown? If so, are people told to watch them in "private viewing booths"? Because that's probably not good.

But of course, the most important determining factor is the philosophy *behind* the class. Here are a few of the most popular:

Lamaze. The Lamaze method burst onto the scene in the fifties, when Dr. Fernand "Johnny Bronco" Lamaze, a pompadoured rebel with a motorcycle and a switchblade, roared into town to show those stuck-up squares what psychoprophylactic obstetrics was really all about. The focus is on building Mommy's confidence through mastery of breathing techniques. Daddy actively participates as Mommy's "coach," meaning he's taught to chew tobacco, yell "Let's see some hustle out there!" and argue with attending physicians until he is ejected from the hospital.

---

* We're looking at you, *The Golden Bowl.*

Bradley. Dr. Robert Bradley based his pioneering method of childbirth on his own boyhood experiences on a farm, watching animals give birth. The emphasis: deep abdominal breathing and self-awareness. The goal: sweet, succulent veal.

International Childbirth Education Association classes. These explore a variety of overseas techniques, such as Germany's *Schimpflickgeburt* (shameful birth) and *hurihuri,* the modern Japanese method that takes forty-five seconds and ends with a junior high school entrance exam.

ALACE (Association of Labor Assistants and Childbirth Educators). A midwifes' group devoted to rejecting medication and embracing the hardship of bearing a child. Mantras include "No pain, no gain!" "Feel the burn!" and, toughest of all, "Now give me ten more!"

Alexander technique. Derived from a method popular in acting schools. Students learn to control posture, relieve stress, and nail that callback for the Vaginex ad.

Hypno-birthing. Particularly effective on women who were hypno-impregnated. It worked for Rosemary!

Home study. Many of the above-mentioned techniques are available on DVD, CD, and vinyl. (Seriously, man, Lamaze breathing exercises sound so much more *authentic* on LP.)

Whichever class you and Mommy end up dragging Daddy kicking and screaming to, remember: Billions of babies have been born without the benefit of a single formal lesson. The purpose of a class is not to make your parents worry about childbirth *more.* It's to make them worry about it *earlier.*

Lamaze International

(NASSAU COUNTY FAMILY CENTER CAMPUS)

By virtue of the authority invested in Kathy, the Instructor, following her one-year part-time distance-education program,

Does hereby by confer upon

Margaret Zipf

and her coach

Spouse

the degree of

Bachelor of Knowing How to Breathe When You're in Labor

Cum Laude

And has granted this diploma as evidence thereof in the State of New York, in the City of Garden City, in the Mall of Roosevelt Field.

Kathy Natazzio,
Kathy Natazzio,
Instructor/Co-owner

Joe Natazzio
Joseph Natazzio
Dean of Studies/Co-owner

CHILDBIRTH-EDUCATION FIGHT SONGS

In childbirth class, as in college, nothing fosters school spirit like a good fight song.

WE WELCOME YOU

We welcome you to birthing school!
We're mighty glad you're here!
Your pregnancy's a private thing
In which we'll interfere!
We'll lock you in!
We'll freak you out!
We'll sow the seeds of fear and doubt!
Please pay by credit card
As you exit the birthing school!

LAMAZE CHEER

Two, four, six, eight!
Two, four, six, eight!
Two, four, six, eight!
Two, four, six, eight!
[Repeat 500 times.]

ODE TO NATURAL CHILDBIRTH

Give me an N!
Give me an A!
Give me a T!
Give me a U!
Give me an R!
Give me a fucking epidural!

TAUNT FOR RIVAL PARENTS

B-A-B-Y!
Yours ain't got no alibi!
He's ugly! Yeah! He's ugly! Yeah!

SPOUSAL CALL-AND-RESPONSE

WIFE: *When I say "Ready," you say "Push!"*
    Ready!
HUSBAND: *What?*
WIFE: *Ready!*
HUSBAND: *Oh, sorry. Push!*
WIFE: *When I say "Steady," you say "Breathe!"*
HUSBAND: *Breathe!*
WIFE: *Wait!*
HUSBAND: *What?*
WIFE: *I didn't say "Steady."*
HUSBAND: *I'm sorry, but this is stupid.*
WIFE: *Maybe you're stupid.*

CHAPTER 9

Month 7

Third Trime's the Charm

R ight around now is when you become "legally viable." Your *required* term is, in the eyes of the law, over. If you really wanted to split, there's not much The Man could do about it. But as eager as you are to start your new life, leaving now would be, in a word, premature. You've done too much good work here in prehab to end up in trouble in some halfway house, unprepared to face the world "out there." Stick with the program a few more months. You'll be stronger for it, and your family will still be waiting for you with open arms, ready to welcome home the *real* you . . . the one who isn't hiding behind walls anymore.

Best Weeks Ever! 28–31

WEEK 28

It's the first week of your final trimester, and judging by the **blinking** and **coughing**, we'd say you're trying to get our attention. We're guessing you want us to notice the additional **grooves in your brain**, indicating your growing intelligence. Well, we notice them, and we congratulate you—if you're a girl. If you're a boy, we're also noticing the start of the **descent of your testes**, and to be honest that kind of undermines any neurological progress you may be making.

WEEK 29

Sorry to change the subject, but it's too bad you can't see what **your mother** is looking like these days. Yowzers! Are they going to get that *Hindenburg* radio-announcer guy to broadcast the delivery?! And did you hear her **belly button pop** just now? With that *doink!* sound effect, like when the Road Runner sticks his tongue out?! Hard to believe she's gonna get almost three months *bigger* than this, isn't it? Anyway, this is just between us. Let's not make her self-conscious.

WEEK 30

It's Week 30, and you're starting to **lose your body hair**. If you think that's a bummer, wait till you see what happens to your hair come *Year* 30. This is also around when Mom and Dad start trying to guess what part of you they feel pushing against her belly. A flat surface may be your back. A hard lump could be your head. A soft squishy bag fill of Plastic Poly Pellets is your hackeysack, and if they tanked your shred while you were bustin' big, serves you right. You were hackey hogging, bro. Don't bogart the footbag.

WEEK 31

We notice you've begun developing an **immune system**. Nice. May we ask, is this because you heard about all the **shots** you'll need to get once you're born? Trying to avoid them, are you? That's what we thought, but unfortunately it's not going to work.

Polio vaccine is something you're just never going to produce on your own, so sooner or later you'll have to bite the bullet and— oh, don't start crying. Come on, you're being a total pussy! What? "Maybe you won't develop an immune system at all then"? Fine, be that way. You're only hurting yourself.

What You May Be Concerned She's Not Concerned About

I'M DREAMING OF A WHITE DISCHARGE

"Now that I've begun REM sleep, I've been having dreams, and they're really weird!"

And they're really normal. In the last trimester, the subconscious mind goes into overdrive, producing imagistic fantasies in which deep-seated fears, anxieties, and personal insecurities are realized. In the case of your mommy, these are called **accurate premonitions**. But in your case, they're called **dreams**, and with the fluid you're swimming in, you're going to wake up moist and clammy after *all* of them.

Such dreams are not only natural, they may be also precocious. Freud believed that dreams reflected neuroses left over from infancy. If that's true, here *you* are with neuroses, and you haven't even *been* an infant yet. A fetus who's already sublimating at a one-year-old level? Sounds like *someone* has a future as an outwardly homophobic closeted Republican!

Some of the most common motifs in fetal dreams include:

- **Getting lost.** "I was in an unfamiliar neighborhood downtown. I tried to get out, but it was very dark and I could only move very slowly. I was terrified and began to cry."

- **Public nudity.** "It was my birthday. People were throwing a party for me in a large public building. I showed up naked. Everyone stared at me. I was humiliated and began to cry."
- **Flying.** "I was flying in the air, hoisted by strong, sturdy hands. A bright light hovered over me. I was overjoyed and began to cry."
- **Being chased.** "Someone was right behind me. I couldn't shake him. He was thirty seconds behind me, and somehow I knew he would be for the rest of my life."
- **Gaining your teeth.** "One by one, for no reason, my teeth were coming in."
- **Falling.** "I was falling through an endless black hole. I was indifferent, but when it was over for some reason I began to cry."
- **Missing an exam.** "I was late for my Apgar test. When I got to the test room, I was completely unprepared and began to cry . . . which got me a perfect score!"

These are just a few of the thousands of variations of fetal dreams—some of them scary but most of them harmless, and all of them far less bizarre and disgusting than the one Daddy keeps having where he's breast-feeding his dead grandmother.

TOO MUCH TOO SOON

"I'm beginning to worry I won't be able to manage my sleeping, my eating, my pooping—and my parents, too."

You're setting up an impossible standard for yourself. *You're not Superbaby.* If you think you'll be able to effortlessly balance screaming your lungs out, sucking Mommy's nipples sore, puking a geyser, pissing a waterfall, shitting a mud slide, alienating the nanny, and keeping your parents up all night every night until their marriage is at the breaking point, you're being unrealistic.

Accept it: You're going to be a lot busier than you were the past nine months. So give yourself a break. The best thing to do is prioritize. If damaging Mommy's sanity is important to you, sleep may have to take a backseat to colic. If looking adorable to passersby is something you can't live without, you'll need to cut back on the spitting up on yourself. Above all, don't strain yourself emotionally. You are far too young and fragile to be expected to love *both* your parents. Choose one. Then express that love through sounds and gestures the other can misinterpret as "typical baby stuff," which is the humane thing to do.

It's natural to want to hit the ground running, but trust us: It's a bad idea. In fact, you should not be allowed to hit the ground in any way. That would be very poor parenting.

PLANNED PARENTEDHOOD

"I hear Mommy is writing up a 'birth plan.' Any drastic changes I should know about? She's not thinking anus now, is she?"

Neither as morbid as a living will nor as cynical as a prenup, the **birth plan** is easily the least depressing of Americans' three attempts to set preconditions on their major life milestones. A growing number of parents are now writing out in advance their preferences for how they'd like the big day to go, on issues ranging from the important (that is, how much pain medication Mommy will use) to the absurd (that is, how much she *thinks* she will). These birth plans are negotiated with doctors and hospitals and, once signed, become legally binding contracts; failure to adhere to the terms therein could subject you, the fetus, to possible civil action.*

---

* This is the origin of the phrase "breech birth."

SIB STORY

"I have an older brother and an older sister. Will there be any jealousy on their part once I'm born?"

(Author's note: This question will be guest-answered by one of the world's leading authorities on this subject, Cain.)

[1] And Adam knew Eve; and she conceived, and bore Cain, and said, I have gotten a man from THE LORD.

[2] And for no good reason, did she then conceive my brother Abel, and bore him, and said, Alas, it doth appear the best part of this one did run down the rift of my loins.

[3] And Cain grew to be a tiller of the ground, having always been partial to tilling; but Abel was a keeper of sheep, and sometimes more than a keeper, if thou knoweth what I mean.

[4] And it came to pass, that Cain brought an offering of most pleasing grain and fruit unto THE LORD; whereas Abel brought the scrawny firstlings of his flock, which were not fit to make lambburgers with, to be honest with thee;

[5] But Abel's offering found respect with THE LORD, and Cain's found no respect with THE LORD.

[6] And Cain was very wroth, because this was typical of the treatment he did always receiveth from THE LORD; for THE LORD did let Abel get away with everything; because Abel was "the little baby"; and Abel had "a cute personality"; and Cain had to look out for Abel as if he was his keeper; and Abel this, and Abel that; Abel Abel Abel Abel Abel.

[7] And so it came to pass, when they were in the field, that Cain delivered unto his brother exactly what was coming unto him.

[8] Therefore, now, if any of thee should see THE LORD, and he inquireth as to Abel's whereabouts, thou knoweth nothing;

[9] And if he should inquireth as to my whereabouts, I was out with friends.

But a birth plan's true value is psychological. There's an old saying: Nothing in life is intimidating if you know going in *exactly* the circumstances under which you would want your perineum massaged. Perhaps nowhere is this more true than in childbirth. A birth plan can give your parents a sense of control by helping them prioritize what's *truly* important. So if the first thing Mommy does after pushing you out is check the box next to "give birth" on the piece of paper she's been holding all through labor, take it as a positive sign. She will clearly be keeping all aspects of your childhood in obsessive, compulsive order.

Rashomon Delivery

Sometimes several people involved in the same birth all devise their own individual plans for the big day.

Mrs. Peggy Bradley

12:00 A.M.–7:00 A.M.	Restful, deep sleep
7:00 A.M.–8:00 A.M.	Comfortable, multiorgasmic lovemaking session with Ted
8:30 A.M.	Mani/pedi
9:00 A.M.	First contraction (it tickles!)
9:01 A.M.	Call Dr. Gupta—he is at the hospital waiting for me with no other patients
9:05 A.M.	Get in car
9:09 A.M.	Arrive at hospital (no traffic!!!)
9:10 A.M.	Enter St. Luke's through hallway strewn with ~~rose tulip~~ lilac petals
9:11 A.M.	Begin hospital paperwork
9:11:30 A.M.	Conclude hospital paperwork
9:15 A.M.	Facial and blowout
10:00 A.M.	Ushered into state-of-the-art private birthing room with Martha Stewart eggshell-blue motif and Laura Ashley bedding

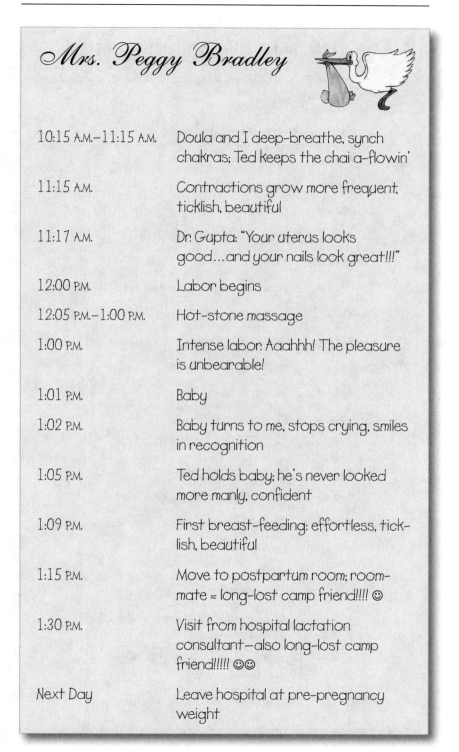

Mrs. Peggy Bradley

10:15 A.M.–11:15 A.M.	Doula and I deep-breathe, synch chakras; Ted keeps the chai a-flowin'
11:15 A.M.	Contractions grow more frequent, ticklish, beautiful
11:17 A.M.	Dr. Gupta: "Your uterus looks good…and your nails look great!!!"
12:00 P.M.	Labor begins
12:05 P.M.–1:00 P.M.	Hot-stone massage
1:00 P.M.	Intense labor. Aaahhh! The pleasure is unbearable!
1:01 P.M.	Baby
1:02 P.M.	Baby turns to me, stops crying, smiles in recognition
1:05 P.M.	Ted holds baby; he's never looked more manly, confident
1:09 P.M.	First breast-feeding: effortless, ticklish, beautiful
1:15 P.M.	Move to postpartum room; roommate = long-lost camp friend!!!! ☺
1:30 P.M.	Visit from hospital lactation consultant—also long-lost camp friend!!!!! ☺☺
Next Day	Leave hospital at pre-pregnancy weight

Mr. Ted Bradley's Birth Plan

9:00 A.M.	Just begin to settle in at work like it's any other day
9:02 A.M.	Phone rings
9:03 A.M.	Oh God oh God oh God
9:05 A.M.	Get in car
9:06 A.M.	Feel overwhelmed
9:08 A.M.	Crash into fruit stand
9:12 A.M.	Attempt to regain composure
9:15 A.M.	Crash into second fruit stand
9:20 A.M.	Enter St. Luke's; puke on ~~rose~~ ~~tulip~~ lilac petals
9:25 A.M.–9:30 A.M.	Help Peggy
9:31 A.M.–9:35 A.M.	Help Peggy help me
9:36 A.M.–9:40 A.M.	Help me help me help me
9:45 A.M.	Bathroom break
10:00 A.M.	Cigarette break
10:15 A.M.	Ativan break
10:30 A.M.	Nervous-breakdown break
11:00 A.M.	Return from original bathroom break
11:00 A.M.–1:00 P.M.	Catatonically obey Peggy, doula, doctors
1:01 P.M.	Baby?!
1:02 P.M.	Baby turns to me, starts crying, screams in disappointment
1:05 P.M.	No no no don't hand him to me! Oh God oh God oh God
1:09 P.M.	First breast-feeding. So long, Peggy's tits, it was nice knowing you
NEXT DAY	Leap of faith into total unknown

DR. JOHN GREENBLATT
Resident in Obstetrics, St. Luke's Hospital

1:00 A.M.	Start fourth consecutive 12-hour shift
1:00 A.M.–10:00 A.M.	Three vaginals, two cesareans, and a VBAC. Sustenance: one bag of cheetos and a Red Bull
10:00 A.M.	Next item on the agenda: Mrs. Bradley and her goddamn baby
10:01 A.M.	Great, she brought along a goddamn doula
10:02 A.M.	Oho! A rare Dr. Gupta sighting! (Mrs. Bradley = rich? Mistress?)
10:30 A.M.	Run into Mr. Bradley in elevator– "Don't be nervous, everything's fine," etc. Seems like putz
11:00 A.M.	Repeat details of Mrs. Bradley's contractions to Gupta like trained fucking seal
11:45 A.M.	Gupta pulls me aside for fifth retelling of "obstetrical residents see 18 holes a week–I play that many every day!" joke
12:00 P.M.	Labor begins. "No epidural." Usual bet with Nurse Pam.
12:04 P.M.	Request for epidural. 4 minutes! Pam owes me dimebag.
12:05 P.M.–1:00 P.M.	Grunting, sweating, pushing, yada yada yada
1:01 P.M.	Baby
1:02 P.M.	That's 12 hours and 2 minutes! Adios, suckers!

FROM THE DESK OF BABY BRADLEY

9:00 A.M.	Stay in womb
10:00 A.M.	Stay in womb
11:00 A.M.	Stay in womb
Rest of day	Stay in womb
Rest of week	Stay in womb
Rest of life	Never, ever, ever leave womb

LOVE ME DOULA

Fig. 39. *This is not Rainbow Crystalpepsi Moonbeamowitz. It's her older, more grounded sister.*

"My parents say they're thinking about getting a doula. Is now really the time to be buying a new car?"

Doulatry has been the subject of many unfair stereotypes over the years. But today's doula—for ease of discussion, we'll call her Rainbow Crystalpepsi Moonbeamowitz—is a dedicated, nurturing, unshaven woman (Fig. 39) who was certified by one of the several birthacademunities in the greater Berkeley area only after a grueling all-morning training session that included no fewer than six group hugs.

If hired, Rainbow's duties will vary, depending on how pushy she is and how needy your mother is. She may help design an entire birth plan complete with worst-case scenarios and alternate endings. She may employ confidence-building techniques like **reflexology**, **aromatherapy**, and **getting Mommy to believe in reflexology and aromatherapy**. Or she may simply offer homemade vegan brownies that taste like beets and sawdust.

> ### UTERINE LINER NOTE
>
> *"Mommy paid that doula three thousand dollars, but it was worth every penny. And yes, I was born yesterday."*
>
> —Ashley Budd, one day old, Chappaqua, New York

But it is at the hospital where the doula really shines. Throughout labor, she will be there to hold Mommy's hand, adjust Mommy's bed, reject Mommy's pleas for an epidural as "unbeautiful," and generally provide her with a voice of experience that the team of highly trained doctors and nurses surrounding her will in no way find intrusive and insulting.

For a doula is guided by a noble belief: that a woman should give birth in a way that is spiritually fulfilling for her, the doula. And that way is drug-free. She believes women in labor have become bullied into taking pain-relief medication solely because it makes them feel so very, very much better. In truth, she argues, a prolonged, agonizing childbirth is Mommy's fundamental right, one that must be defended against all who would deny it—including, by Hour 16, Mommy herself.

If Mommy is interested in finding a doula, she can ask her practitioner, or just swing by any kiosk at Mount Holyoke. A warning: Doulas can charge anywhere from five hundred to fifteen hundred dollars, so they're not for the very poor . . . only the very needy.

A Fetal Examination®
PREGNANCY AND THE INTERNET: THE WORLD WIDE WOMB

The **Internet** is a miraculous parallel universe in which every conceivable fact or opinion is simultaneously true, false, and related to Katie Holmes. This is certainly true in the field of obstetrics. A few short centuries ago, women's understanding of pregnancy derived largely from what little alarmist, contradictory, spiteful hearsay they painstakingly pieced together over the course of their lives. Now, thanks to the miracle that is the World Wide Web, all that hearsay can be found at the click of a button!

It's true that the Web has yet to change the *process* of birthing the way it has other activities, like masturbating and shopping while masturbating. The dot-com bubble of the nineties saw several failed attempts to transform pregnancy via the Internet, most notably **E-ject**, which promised, "through streamlined programmatics and piggybacked shareware," to make gestation last four days. As for the swift rise and fall of **amiviableornot.com**, the less said the better.

Fig. 40. *Fetal blogs are not yet wireless.*

But the Web *has* succeeded as a method of creative expression and community building. Thousands of young voices now begin their literary journeys on **fetal blogs** (Fig. 40); others can't go a day without uploading their innermost thoughts and feelings onto **YouFallopianTube**. Sites like **Pre-facebook** allow fetuses to reconnect with old friends, while those looking for new

Common Pregnancy
Chat-Room Abbreviations

IVF	in vitro fertilization
ZIFT	zygote intrafallopian transfer
OMG!	Oh my gynecologist!
TTC	trying to conceive
TTCHSB	trying to conceive, husband shooting blanks
SHJWIDTHWTSF	shit, he just walked in; don't tell him what that stood for
SAHM	stay-at-home mom
WAHM	work-at-home mom
RAHM	Barack Obama's chief of staff
LOL	lots of lactating
LMAO	lactating my ass off
ROTFLMAO	rolling on the floor lactating my ass off
IMHO	I miss having orgasms
2wp	2 weeks pregnant
2mp	2 months pregnant
2yp	I am an African elephant
TWDB	typing while delivering baby

Point and Kick!

Be sure to check out whattoexpectwhenyoureexpected.com. It's got great features, like a list of more than forty thousand baby names. Pick your favorite one! The odds of winding up with it are as small as you are!

friends can browse popular matchmaking services to meet, mingle, and arrange postpartum playdates.

Of course, this entire discussion is probably a little too technical for you. The cruel fact is the Internet can only be used and understood by people of a certain age, and . . . frankly, as a third-trimester fetus, you're way too old. Don't worry about it, Grandma. If anything important happens, we'll call you on your rotary phone.

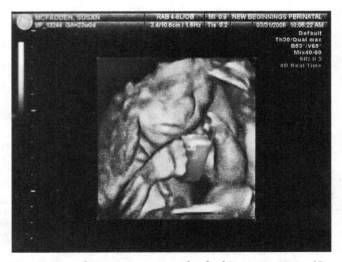

Fig. 41. *One of America's most popular fetal Twitterers, Peter (Or Possibly Mark) McFadden will be retiring at birth to spend more time with his family.*

Pregnancy chat rooms are valuable resources for mommies, the-oretically. Below, a sample page from citymommy.com.

[-] 6mp = still safe to fly on plane this weekend? wndrngmom   6 REPLIES

EXPECTING, GENERAL TOPICS, IRRESPONSIBLE PARENTING

[REPLY | WATCH | OPTIONS]

>> yes if you r a horrible person schadenfraud08 [REPLY | OPTIONS]

>> depends what airline my cousin flew Delta and had premature labur

newwifestales [REPLY | OPTIONS]

>> It's really up to you. nohelpatall [REPLY | OPTIONS]

>> It's right on the cusp of what is considered safe, so
you should only fly if you're going to visit Howard
Stern bababuey bababuey babanuey bababuey!
Hnkngrydrnkndwrf [REPLY | OPTIONS]

[-] Am Svetlana to hire for nanny I apply. To be loving all children except when
they are bad then to beat with stiff reeds. Svetlanananny@yahoo.com. Please to
provide reeds.   0 REPLIES

[-] Are scented candles safe during pregnancy? Funkycat24   5 REPLIES

EXPECTING, GENERAL TOPICS, IRRESPONSIBLE PARENTING

[REPLY | WATCH | OPTIONS]

>> no and your screen name is stupid schadenfraud08   [REPLY | OPTIONS]

>> depends what scent my cousin used lavender and had low birth-
weight newwifestales [REPLY | OPTIONS]

>> Research on this subject is inconclusive. nohelpatall
[REPLY | OPTIONS]

[-] You want Hispanic nannies? We got Hispanic nannies! World's largest
selection. Colombians, Dominicans, Ecuadorians, Panamanians, Puerto Ricans,
Venezuelans—if they're dusky and love babies, we've got 'em in stock!
VITOSHOUSEOFHISPANICNANNIES.COM. No habla español.   1 REPLY

[–] I'm considering giving birth at County General. Any good/bad experiences?

Laurag4765   3 REPLIES

EXPECTING, DELIVERY, UNSUBSTANTIATED RUMORS

[REPLY | WATCH | OPTIONS]

>> Just search it on the boards dumbass **schadenfraud08**

[REPLY | OPTIONS]

>> Had both of my kids there. That was years ago, though. **nohelpatall**

[REPLY | OPTIONS]

[–] Name Poll: Tiffany, Fantasia or Madison? **1moreontheway96**   7 REPLIES

EXPECTING, DUBIOUS NOMENCLATURE

[REPLY | WATCH | OPTIONS]

>> depends do u want her to be stripper, porn star or whore

schadenfraud08   [REPLY | OPTIONS]

>> or all three at once **snarkymom**   [REPLY | OPTIONS]

>> Yes! **nohelpatall**   [REPLY | OPTIONS]

>> I like tiffany . . . but I'm biased! **tiffanythestripper**   [REPLY | OPTIONS]

CHAPTER 10

Month 8

Allow Six to Eight Weeks for Delivery

In little over a month, you will have the monopoly on cuteness in your family. (Older siblings? Their charm mortgage forecloses the second your head pokes through.) But for now, your parents are adorable! You should see them together in your room—painting, planning, arranging itsy-bitsy furniture, having "serious" talks about "budgets" and "sharing the responsibility." Just like real grown-ups! And the things they come up with! Just now, Mommy said, "You won't complain about alternating night feedings, will you?" And then Daddy said, "Of course not. I will relish that bonding time." Oh, if only they could stay that naïve!

Best Weeks Ever! 32–35

WEEK 32

You are a goddamn lazy-ass. Look at you, **sleeping 90 to 95 percent of the time**. *When are you going to do something with your* *life!?* Mommy's ribs ain't gonna kick themselves! On the plus side, good news on the dermatological front: Your **wrinkles** are disappearing, and your **skin is no longer transparent**. That's good. For a while there, you were giving off a real Slim Good-body vibe. Ever see that guy? Had his insides painted on his unitard? Sang a lot? Creepy as hell.

WEEK 33

What's your favorite position? Ours is reverse cowboy. Guess yours is **head down**, **bottom up**, since that's how you appear to be aligning yourself. A little conventional, frankly, but then again it's popular for a reason. Breech births are not only riskier but less picturesque. For Mommy, the highlight of her pregnancy experience will be your little head emerging from her vagina . . . a vagina that, in all likelihood, hasn't experienced a little head in a long, long time.

WEEK 34

Mom is passing on **antibodies** to you. They're very friendly chemicals. Just don't get them started on **bodies**. They fucking *hate* them. And congratulations, gentlemen: After a careful, controlled descent, it appears your **testes** have safely touched down on Planet Scrotum. Wondering what they're for? To provide hours of endless entertainment to you—and, when struck, to others.

WEEK 35

You're feeling cramped in there, and no wonder: You're **five pounds** of *carne* in a three-pound empanada. And a lot of that meat ain't exactly lean. You're up to **15 percent body fat**, and

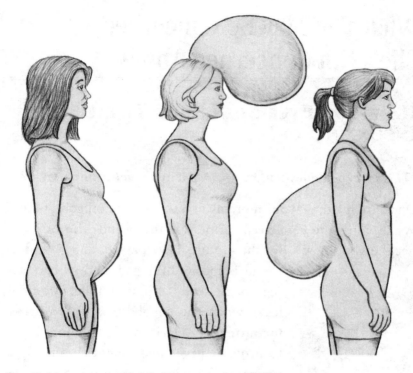

Fig. 42. *Mommies carry their babies in a number of different ways.*

you're getting chubbier by the hour. But your brain is developing at an astonishing rate. Putting all your energy into your mind, not your body, huh? All right, Poindexter. Just don't come crying to us when the jocks release greased pigs in the Tri-Lam frat! NERRRRRRRRRRRRRRD!

What You May Be Concerned She's Not Concerned About

HAVE YOU EVER SEEN SUCH TOTAL INCONTINENCE?

"This is an odd question, but . . . Mommy's toilet trained, right?"

Once upon a time, your mommy and **urine** were on good terms. When you were conceived, urine was the friend who brought her the good news. But the months have passed, and now that

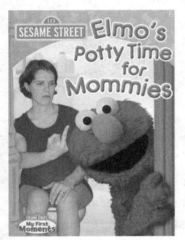

Fig. 43.

friend is loose, unhinged, and embarrassing to be seen with in public. Mommy leaks when she coughs or laughs (**stress incontinence**), feels overwhelming urges to urinate (**urge incontinence**), and wets her pants in front of large groups of people (**hilarious incontinence**).

The solution? **Potty training**. Now is the time for you or (if necessary) some other family member to step up and supervise Mommy's long, slow struggle for bladder control. There are any number of books, DVDs, and websites specifically focused on this issue, but here are a few tips:

- Set up a reward system. Every time Mommy pees in the potty, she gets a gold star. Every time Mommy goes a whole day without an accident, she gets a Marc Jacobs black leather handbag with his signature buckles.
- After a trip to the potty, watch Mommy for indications that she will need to pee again very soon. One such indication: She is still pregnant.

- Work around situations that tend to provoke her peeing. For example, if she pees when she laughs, Daddy should turn on *Family Guy*.
- Above all, be patient! Accidents *will* happen. Panty liners *will* be saturated. The seating area at Pizzeria Uno *will* get dampened. But the effort is worth it. Even if Mommy's forty, bladder control is a skill that, once learned, she will have for the rest of her decade.

YOU'RE CUT OUT FOR THIS

"Mommy says she's open to the idea of a 'C-section.' Isn't it risky adding a bridge to a song that already has a verse and a chorus?"

O hypothetical reader, with your wacky misunderstandings! No, the C in this case stands for "Caesarean," and a **Caesarean section** is an alternate form of delivery in which a baby is removed from the uterus via incisions in her mommy's abdomen. Throughout history, C-sections have been used when vaginal birth endangered the well-being of the baby or the mother. Today, they are used

Fig. 44. *The "Caesarean section" was also the area in the Colosseum reserved for personal guests of Caesar. The ancient equivalent of a luxury box, it featured a private vomitorium and complimentary felching.*

when Mommy is a week from full term and has an invite to the Karl Lagerfeld show in Milan next Friday.

C-sections have never been more popular. Advances in technology have made them safe, quick, and, if Mommy asks the anesthesiologist for "something trippy," pretty damn fun. They're a particularly prudent choice for bigger and older women, though even young, fit mommies see the appeal of not spending their first week postpartum applying chilled witch hazel to their

Fig. 45. *The "Caesarean section" was also the group nickname for the writing staff for* Your Show of Shows. *It included Neil Simon, Mel Brooks, Larry Gelbart, and Carl Reiner and was the inspiration for the movie* My Favorite Year *and the play* Everybody Shut the Fuck Up!

assholes. We should also mention the ongoing debate over **VBAC** (vaginal birth after Caesarean). Some doctors say it's feasible, but others question the need for it, since the baby's already been born, so why stuff him back in there just to do it again a different way?

If you are delivered by C-section, you may feel somewhat disappointed. It's like scoring tickets to the Oscars, then being told at the last minute you'd have to enter through a side door. Maybe it's more "convenient," but what about the red carpet . . . the bright lights . . . the gowns . . . the strangers grabbing for a piece of you . . . the chance to actually have an answer to the question "Who are you wearing?" Well, here's the thing: *You're going to the Oscars!* Isn't that the point? Just be thankful you get to experience it at all. It's a hell of a spectacle, and who knows? Maybe you'll wind up sitting next to the Mambo King himself, Antonio Banderas (Fig. 47)!

Fig. 46. *The "Caesarean section" is also the portion of the* Planet of the Apes *films dedicated to the future ape rebellion led by Caesar (Roddy McDowall). That concludes the third and final variation on this joke. Thank you for sticking with it.*

Fig. 47. *Seriously, can you imagine sitting next to Antonio Banderas at the Oscars? How cool would that be?*

SHOWER GRAPES

"I hear a lot of women's voices, the sound of crinkling wrapping paper, and cheesy songs from the 1980s. Where am I?"

You are at Mommy's **shower**, named for what she will want to spend an hour in immediately afterward to scrub off all the bullshit.

By tradition baby showers are women-only, a policy strenuously objected to by as many as zero men. The guests are Mommy's female relatives, friends, classmates, and co-workers, each of whom now has a chance to verify the vicious stories Mommy has told about the others. The event is usually organized by Mommy's best and/or least creatively fulfilled friend. The food often has a theme, like "nursery rhymes," or "fairy tales," or "crap I wouldn't feed my cat." Guests generally play pregnancy-related games. A common activity is attempting to cut string to the exact diameter of Mommy's belly. The one who comes closest gets to leave.

The party culminates with the public opening of the presents. These presents were chosen not to be useful, but *to be publicly opened.* No one wants to be seen as the boring old fuddy-duddy who buys new mothers practical things like diapers and burp cloths. Instead they come bearing gift-wrapped Limoges porcelain ladybug-shaped keepsake boxes that do Mommy a favor by breaking on the drive home.

Through it all, Mommy will smile bravely, oohing and ahhing, enduring a brutal half hour "mouth Kegel" that will leave her upper lips as well toned as her lower ones. But somewhere down the line she'll be glad she went. This was her last planned group get-together before her delivery, and later on, she'll realize how well its endless, oppressive tedium prepared her for your first few months of life.

PREVENTING MISMARRIAGE

"Lately Mommy and Daddy have been fighting a lot. Is it my fault?"

What a silly question! When parents fight, it's *always* the kid's fault.

Back when Mommy and Daddy were a twosome, they could devote all their energy and affection to each other. There was no one else to demand their attention or keep them up all night. (Yes, there was Melissa, but that was just a couple of times, and it was more experimenting than anything else.) But all that will change once their first child comes along. You will be their bundle of joy, yes, but also their intruder, their wedge, a thief in their house of love. Their marriage will transition out of its first, or "fun," stage into an unknown new one; and while they don't yet know *exactly* what this will entail, they are starting to suspect it will involve fewer Pixies concerts and more exploded-diaper disinfectant sessions.

The emotions caused by this realization have made things tense. It's normal. Hopefully, Mommy and Daddy will begin to reconnect by setting aside time once a week from now until your birth to go out and do something as a couple. A movie, a romantic dinner, one last Pixies concert—anything to remind them of why they fell in love, got married, had a wonderful couple of years, then decided to push their luck. If they invest the time in their relationship now, it'll make all the difference when "baby makes three." Otherwise, Daddy's out the door when baby *is* three.

A Fetal Examination®

BREAST-FEEDING: YOU WILL SUCK

Mammals are the most advanced life-form on earth. They are named for tits. This gives you some small sense of just how wondrous breasts really are. Renowned for eons for their remarkable ability to give men erections, breasts have in recent decades

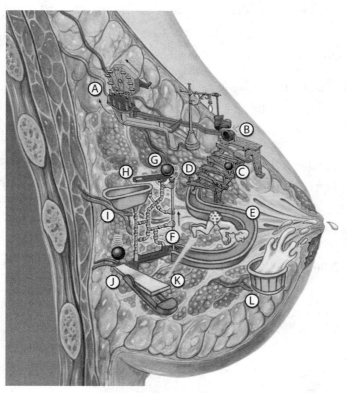

Fig. 48. *Lactation is the end product of billions of years of evolution. Shortly after delivery, the body produces the hormone prolactin, which turns the crank (A), which tips the bucket (B), which holds the metal ball (C), which rolls down a staircase (D) and along a groove (E), tipping the bowling ball (F) into the bathtub (G), to fall onto the diving board (H), catapulting a diver (I) into a wash tub (J), splashing breast milk out of the nipple. (Diagram courtesy American Medical Association)*

Further Reflexion

Sucking and rooting are two of the many involuntary actions you can look forward to being born without any control over. Others:

◆ **Plantar ("Babinski") reflex.** Stroking your foot from heel to toe will prompt you to flare your toes upward, turn your feet in, and yell "Babinski!"

◆ **Startle ("Moro") reflex.** A loud noise or feeling of falling will prompt you to extend your limbs, arch your back, and clench your fists. Then you will exhale, mistakenly believing you were imagining things. In fact, the killer is right behind you.

◆ **Walking reflex.** Being held upright on a flat surface will prompt you to lift one leg, then the other. It's a reflex. You're not walking yet. Don't get excited, Baryshnikov.

◆ **Fencing reflex.** Being placed on your back will prompt you to assume a "fencing position"—that is, head to one side, opposite limbs flexed, masked, attached to a wire, thrusting an épée at your parents.

◆ **Kitsch reflex.** Being put into a tiny adorable animal costume will prompt you to cringe in shame.

BREAST MILK: A STANDARD TASTING MENU

COURSE	NOTES
Foremilk	So-called "thirst quencher"—smooth, easy-drinking, beechwood-aged
Hindmilk	Rich; high in fat; full-bodied; bold finish; notes of lactose, antibody, citrus
Mainmilk	Other breast often comes with sidemilk
Circummilk	Requires 360-degree tongue motion around nipple; first consumed by Magellan
Harveymilk	Makes you courageous, San Franciscan, gay
Cheese course	A.k.a. "spit-up"
Brunchmilk	[Available Sundays 10:00 A.M.–4:00 P.M.]

"stepped into their own" with a new emphasis on their long-forgotten secondary function: feeding infants. Indeed, piles of research long ago showed scientists there's no improving on natural breast milk.*

We're bringing this topic up now because it may take some getting used to. Right now the idea of **breast-feeding** may seem foreign to you, since you've never seen a **breast**, or **fed**. But you'll be amazed at how natural the whole thing will feel. First, you'll innately recognize the breasts as the twin spheroid ventrally symmetrical sudoriferous protuberances guys go nuts for. Then your instincts will kick in: Within minutes of your birth, a **rooting reflex** will help you turn your head breastward, a **sucking re-**

---

* So they've shifted their focus to improving on natural breasts. Which they have. *Spectacularly.*

Fig. 49. *This picture serves no legitimate purpose whatsoever.*

flex will help you extract the milk, and a **taunting reflex** will help you act just awkward and fussy enough to convince Mommy she's doing it all wrong. But she's not—and you've just entered flavor country!

From your standpoint as a consumer, the advantages of breast-feeding are many:

It's personalized. Breast milk contains more than one hundred ingredients not found in cow's milk or baby formula, including proteins, amino acids, and love. Its composition even changes over the course of a single fifteen-minute meal to provide balance and variety (see chart, previous page).

It keeps you thin. Breast-feeding puts *you,* not a bottle, in control of portion size, so you stop eating when you're no longer hungry. This is in contrast to your parents, who as typical adult Americans only stop eating when they can no longer leave the house without greasing the door frame.

It goes down—and comes out—easy. Infants who nurse are rarely constipated; their feces comes out loose, free, and redolent of patchouli. Plus, it's much less likely to cause diaper rash, so you can *finally* feel healthy and confident wallowing in your own filth.

It's safe. No one is born allergic to his mother's breast milk. *That's* not how they poison you.

It promotes the unconscious differentiation of the "primordial object" into a breast-as-nourisher versus breast-as-erotic-object dichotomy, forming a lifelong anaclitic Oedipal complex marked

by unabreactable fetishizations of vampirism, oral sadism, and cannibalism. Self-explanatory.

It's cheap. Free, in fact. If Mommy tries charging you, she's grifting. Remember: There's no such thing as a "nipple tax."

Fig. 50. *The 1970s saw the emergence of "blactation consultants" offering advice for women . . . and payback for The Man.*

It gives Daddy an excuse to sleep all night. No trivial point. It's in your best interest to live a lifestyle promoting "sleep inequity" between your parents. The resulting anger, resentment, and mutual recrimination will be all the evidence you need to show you're making a difference in their lives.

It makes you the center of attention. Public breast-feeding has emerged as a political issue in recent years. Many Americans, particularly men, are repulsed by the sight of a woman offering her ripe bosom to a cradled infant for suckling, even if others found that last clause alone reason enough to drop this book and head for www.milfsquirters.com. In response, several so-called "lactivist" groups have emerged demanding that nursing mothers be given respect, tolerance, and a float in the Saint Patrick's Day Parade. It's a touchy subject. But no matter what the other diners at Le Bernardin think as they watch you greedily hovering six inches over Mommy's vanilla flan, this much is certain: You will be noticed!

Fig. 51. *European attitudes toward public breast-feeding are liberal, as evidenced by Amsterdam's famous Wet Nurse District.*

BOTTLE FEEDING: ALMOST LIKE LOVE

Don't despair if your parents wind up feeding you formula from a bottle. It provides several non-disadvantages.

Longer satisfaction. Formula takes longer to digest than breast milk. This extends the period between feedings, so you'll see your Mommy less, which is for the best, since she's clearly sickened by your touch.

More Daddy. Bottle feeding means you'll be spending some quality feeding time with Daddy. That's good. Maybe *he'll* like you.

Some third advantage that we couldn't think of. Because lists have to have three things on them.

Popular Breast-Feeding Positions

The Jawbreaker

The Keg Stand

The Goin' Back to Kali

The FDR

The Bizarre Side Effect

CHAPTER 11

Month 9
Paradise Almost Lost

C an it be? Yes, it could. Something's comin'. Something good. (Icky, but good.) All those months of hard work lying around are about to pay off. Excited? Wigged out, more likely: Surveys show that moving is one of the most stressful experiences in a person's life. But you don't have much stuff, and while the place you've been crashing at is a good starter home, you've pretty much outgrown it. As for your house, talk about opulent—it even has a separate room to go poopy in!

Best Weeks Ever! 36–40

WEEK 36

You look ripped, man. The quads, the traps, the pecs . . . you have been doing some serious body building! But there's one piece of equipment you've been neglecting: your **digestive system**. Consider giving it a "warm-up," as you'll be exercising it fairly vigorously for the next century or so. Start slow: Ingest . . . exgest. Ingest . . . exgest. By the way, smart move shaving off that body hair. It really highlights your— What? You didn't shave it? You **swallowed it along with some amniotic fluid to form your first bowel movement**? Hmmm. Bet that went over *great* in the locker room.

WEEK 37

As of this week, you are considered **full term**. Think of the next few weeks as like that weird limbo period after you get into college but before you graduate high school. Does that analogy make sense? No? Well, kudos anyway. And **refraining from letting your skull plates fuse together** . . . well, it means a lot to Mom. It reduces from ninth to eighth the circle of hell that pushing you out will feel like.

WEEK 38

This week, your body is producing a lot of **surfactant**, fluid that prevents the air sacs in the lungs from . . . oh, you don't care about this stuff anymore. Actually, here's a better analogy than the high school one: Remember the time between Obama's election and his inauguration? When no one gave a crap anymore what Bush was doing, even Bush? Well, right now, this pregnancy is President Bush. If he wants to create some last-minute surfactant or pardon some cronies, fine. It doesn't matter. In a few weeks, you can bet your sweet ass you're going to see some change you can believe in.

WEEK 39

On second thought, that paragraph was unfair. Not to Bush, but to all that you've accomplished over the last nine months. So let's use this, your penultimate week in the womb, to look back fondly on these thirty-eight eventful Best Weeks Ever: the personal growth—the cell-splitting hilarity—the heart-forming emotion—the unforgettable experiences you will never remember. Oh sure, there were some rough patches, but you wouldn't have had it any other way. Because when it came to your fetal ontogeny . . . you didn't want to miss a thing. [*Cut to montage of your development from zygote to full term, accompanied by Aerosmith's "I Don't Want to Miss a Thing."*]

Week 40

Well, that's all for "Best Weeks Ever!" Before we go, we'd like to acknowledge the one person who made it all possible: **you**. You've let us peek "behind the scenes" to reveal intimate details about your life others would have been too dignified to reveal. So on behalf of everyone involved in this production—Mommy, Daddy, Dr. Rosenblatt, Dr. Nath after Dr. Rosenblatt was arrested—we want to thank you for letting us share this pivotal moment of your life with you. We wish you the very best of luck. Good night.

Week 41

Uh . . . did you hear us? Pregnancy's over. You don't have to be born, but you can't stay here. Good night.

Week 42

Dude, get the fuck out.

What You May Be Concerned She's Not Concerned About

GENERATION NEST

"She's Swiffering the ceiling again."

Sad to say, Mommy is in the grip of one of Mother Nature's most powerful impulses—the **nesting instinct**. It can be seen in the mother eagle, building her aerie to form a perfect circle; the expectant house cat, hoarding soft cloth to line her nook; and the brood mare, bedecking her unborn foal's stable with wall art from the Crate & Barrel catalogue.

In their case, it's cute. In Mommy's, it's pathological. The woman you know and love has been replaced by an obsessive-compulsive zombie. The laid-back chick Daddy used to sleep till noon with is unrecognizable. In fact, he's become her enabler, sent out at all hours with loose twenties to score "sponge," "brush" or "Tide powder." Put simply, Mommy is a cleaning and organizing addict, and *nothing*—not you, not insomnia, not even utter pointlessness—can keep her from getting hopped up on Windex.

As heartbreaking as it is, Mommy's addiction may only stop when she hits rock bottom—that is, when she scrubs the house down to its granite foundation. But to expedite that process, you might want to consider an **intervention**. The sudden sight of you—ideally alongside Daddy, other loved ones, and a team of medical professionals—might just shock her into realizing that she can't go on like this. But a word of warning: This course of action is not for the reticent. *Voice your unhappiness the second you see her.*

> **UTERINE LINER NOTE**
>
> *"I didn't think it was possible, but my mother just alphabetized the furniture by height."*
>
> —James Petersen, Week 39, Etobicoke, Ontario

SHE CAN TAKE IT WITH YOU

"Mom and Dad have set aside what they're taking to the hospital. Can you recommend a good moving company?"

Sounds like they might have done a little **overpacking**. It's a common problem for soon-to-be parents; they tend to go overboard, realizing that this is the last chance they'll have to pack for an overnight trip for at least three years. Here's a checklist of items they *should* bring:

- ❐ You
- ❐ Ten *notarized* copies of the birth plan (*N.B.: By law, unnotarized birth plans are invalid!*)
- ❐ Two copies of this book—one for reference, one to bite through during labor
- ❐ Comfortable shoes (heels no higher than four inches)
- ❐ Change of life priorities and/or underwear
- ❐ Basic toiletries
- ❐ Advanced toiletries (for experienced birth-givers only)
- ❐ Back-rub needs (oil, rolling pin, incredibly sore back)
- ❐ A watch with a second hand for timing how long it takes Daddy to lose interest in timing Mommy's contractions
- ❐ Entertainment (any DVD with Antonio Banderas should do the trick!)
- ❐ Snacks for her, Daddy . . . *and everyone else in the room* (it's only fair)
- ❐ An iPod, preferably with music on it
- ❐ Video recorder/still camera/daguerrotype machine/ stereopticon/easel and set of paints
- ❐ Her favorite pillow
- ❐ Her least favorite pillow (for placement under ass)
- ❐ Maxi-maxi-maxi pads (recommended brand: Stayfree® Ultra-sponge Longs with Beach Towel Wings)

❐ Nursing panties

❐ A "Who to Call" list

❐ A "Who to Forget to Call, Thereby Straining the Relationship" list

❐ Private-school applications

MATERNITY HORDE

"To the nearest hundred, how many people should Mommy invite to my birth?"

A growing trend in recent years is inviting an ever larger group of friends and family to the delivery room. But until recently, women wishing to *entertain* while bearing young could do little more than host a small mid-birth cocktail party. Now, with advances in medico-tainment technology, your arrival can be celebrated in person by up to five hundred people. And with more and more hospitals offering catering services—and more and more catering halls offering maternity wards—the birth party, or **extractvaganza**, is rapidly becoming an accepted part of the natal process. Such a party can require months of planning and cost more than $100,000; but for a couple about to bring a new life into the world, what better use of their time and money could there possibly be?

If your parents do throw such a party, your role in planning it will be somewhat limited. But there are a few points of etiquette to keep in mind:

+ The bar is open-breast.
+ At some point, Mommy will begin gently rocking you. This is your first dance. The music will be "Unchained Melody," "The Way You Look Tonight," or "Baby Got Back." Creepy? Oh yes.

- One of Daddy's friends may suddenly stand up and begin roasting you. Pay him no mind. He is drunk, and most of his ribald anecdotes about your "origin" are half-truths at best.

- A tradition: A group of Mommy's single friends will gather. Mommy will turn around and throw the placenta over her head toward them. By tradition, whoever catches it will be the next woman to Purell her hands.

- Above all, keep in mind that your parents will be showing you off to hundreds of people, so even though you'll have just been born five minutes ago, it would mean a lot to them if you could quit with the crying and maybe smile a little.

THE RUPTURE IS NIGH

"I'm thinking about breaking Mommy's water. Could you let me know when she's in the supermarket?"

That *would* be hilarious! But unnecessary. Only 10 to 15 percent of pregnant women experience pre-labor membrane rupture. Most are already at the hospital by the time they start leaking labor liquor, and even those who *do* seep sac syrup tend to merely *drip* womb juice, rather than gush out a whole geyser of baby brine.

But this period does offer another option for gross-stuff-coming-out-of-Mommy's-vagina fans: The **mucous plug** (Fig. 52). It's done a great job keeping her cervix (and you) bacteria-free all these months, but now it's in

Fig. 52. *The picture of a mucous plug that was originally here was removed after it sickened five workers at our printing press.*

your way, just as Mommy herself will be by the time you're fif-teen. So out it goes, either gradually or as a small clump of quasi-sashimi in the toilet. Soon another mucousy clump will emerge, this one pinkish or red. It's called **bloody show**, and if made properly it will also contain horseradish. It's a pretty sure sign that labor is about to begin, but don't worry: Mommy still has enough time to remove, isolate, and exorcise those panties.

Other common pre-labor symptoms include increased pelvic pressure, more frequent Braxton Hicks contractions, and having had enough of this fucking shit already.

YOU OR FALSE?

"Mommy thinks she's in labor, but I know from an inside source—me—that she's not."

You sly dog! You must be taking part in that beloved hazing ritual known as **false labor**. For the uninitiated, that's when a first-time Mommy's unborn baby and husband conspire, through uterine motion and exaggerated alarmism, to "falsely" convince her she's in labor. Once she's at the hospital, the med-ical staff (all of whom are also in on the joke) put her through the wringer, keeping her fooled for hours, stifling their tittering even as the attending doctor wonders aloud if she might need "a Caesarean salad," the hospital PA keeps paging "Dr. Liza Lott," and the nurses all simultaneously don Groucho Marx glasses.

False labor lasts four or five hours, depending on how much fun everyone's having laughing at Mommy. It usually ends with her ObGyn emerging from behind a curtain and shouting, "Smile—you just went through *false* labor!" Mommy groans, sighs, says something like "You got me!" and goes home wiser, and with some lovely parting gifts.

The Five Stages of Pre-Labor Grief

Neonatal psychologists have identified five stages people go through in the process of dealing with leaving the womb.

1. **Denial:** "No way! I'm going to gestate here fifty years! My grandkids will be visiting me in this womb!"
2. **Anger:** "It's not fair! This is Dr. Miller's fault! He's the one who assigned me a due date!"
3. **Bargaining:** "Just let me stay here long enough to get a tooth."
4. **Depression:** "I'll just sit here and let Mommy's pelvic muscles carry me where they may."
5. **Acceptance:** "It'll be okay. At least I'll get to pee in Daddy's face."

COME OUT, COME OUT, WHENEVER YOU ARE

"I was due five days ago, but I'm not budging. If Mommy wants me, she's going to have to sweeten the deal."

First of all, the bad news. Are you lying down? The doctors have come back with their test results, and it's conclusive: You have, at most, a week before you live. It's scary, no question, but in these final hours you need to make peace with the idea of birth. It's not something to fear. It's just another part of life. All you have to do is follow the light and make a peaceful crossing over to "the other side," where you'll be united with family and loved ones you haven't seen in forever.

Now, you might be wondering why those loved ones—your parents in particular—are so concerned that you're late. After all, didn't this whole process start when *Mommy* was late forty weeks ago? But this is a little different. Not only are Mom and Dad more than ready to welcome you into their lives, but from where Mommy's sitting, *you hurt.* A lot. She gets it: You're a very heavy unborn person living in her tummy who makes it very difficult for her to do anything. Point taken. Let's move on, shall we?

As noted, birth is inevitable. But over the years, a number of methods of **inducing** you to come out have emerged. They are all effective, in the same way that a hypothetical method of inducing Tuesday to occur would inevitably prove effective in less than a week's time. Among the most popular:

- **Walking.** This is the most logical method, based on the well-thought-out principle that when you walk, you, you know, move things around down there, so it probably, like, stimulates stuff.
- **Castor oil.** Guaranteed to make *something* come out *somewhere.*
- **Nipple stimulation.** Releases oxytocin but can lead to painfully long contractions; should only be administered by a board-certified purple-nurplist.
- **Induction.** Through the power of suggestion, the "induction" of labor can be triggered by Mom's simultaneous "induction" into a Hall of Fame. (Note: This technique only works if Mom chooses a career that has a Hall of Fame, devotes her life to being one of the best in the world at it, then retires *exactly* five years before the day she wants you to be born.)
- **Blue cohosh and black cohosh.** Stimulant herbs. Also known for their work at the Seventy-first Annual Academy Awards, which they co-hoshed.
- **Sex.** See "Ask an Old Wife," next page.

Ask an Old Wife

Q: Is it true that sex can induce labor?

A: O hot buttered Jehoshaphat, who cares? Dost thou truly need such an excuse to desire a rigorous fucking? Is not a thorough encuntment by a monstrous piston its own reward? Ah, Josiah my dearest, how I have missed the sensation of thy man-root burrowing into me lo these thirty-six years of barren widowhood! No picklock to open me—no sweet prick to suckle—naught to do but devote that unspent energy to the creation and dissemination of homespun homilies of the most dubious veracity! Damn thee, reader, for thy hot-blooded fruitfulness! Damn thee, and damn thee for thy question!

A Fetal Examination®
NAMES: YOU SHOULD HEAR WHAT THEY'RE CALLING YOU

What's "in"? A name! Assigning newborns a first, or "given," name has never been more popular. Recent estimates suggest that over 95 percent of people ages zero to five are now known by something more specific than "You!"

Your name has no doubt been the subject of much discussion between your parents. He likes Zoe; *she* thinks it sounds precious. She likes Samantha; *he* thinks it sounds quaint. They both like Morgan; *the world* thinks it sounds stupid. So, Morgan it is! That's the thing about your name: It's essentially genetic, deter-

Fig. 53. *The ultimate baby-name resource,* 208,827,064,576 Best Baby Names *lists all 26^8 possible combinations of letters forming a string of eight or less. "Frzhgrrd"? "Grrrq"? "Ethanmup"? They're all in there!*

mined by your parents as surely as your DNA. And though you may one day *legally* change it, in your heart you will remain the same adorable newborn whose parents held you in their arms and repeated the phrase "Hewwo, wizzu Maximus!" over and over again.

But today's parent has an additional challenge: the economy. The naming industry is going through a downturn brought about by the irresponsible speculation of a few years ago, when upscale parents invested in complex derivative names of dubious value. Valeria, Jaden, Kylie—these names are now synonymous with bad names. The spectacular failure of such frivolous nomenclature caused a chain reaction that ultimately threatened the entire naming system itself. Even solid blue chips like Michael and Emily found their value plummeting, and survived only after President Obama restored confidence in them by buying two goldfish and calling them that.

On the plus side, today's Javon Q. Public now has a formidable array of naming helpers at his disposal. This can be seen most dramatically at your local Barnes 'n' Borders, whose "Family" section contains more than a dozen titles consisting of little more than lists of thousands of names (Fig. 53).

It's staggering to ponder the creativity of the authors who could make up so many. Even the handful of names that are *not* entirely original are recontextualized in helpful subcategories. Pat, for example, will be listed under "Irish," "gender-neutral," and "back-related en-

> **UTERINE LINER NOTE**
>
> *"A great name is the difference between self-confidence and a lifetime of shame."*
>
> —Name withheld upon request

couragements." One thing's for sure: *In no way* is the annual sale of millions of these books a scam of the highest order.

A brief glimpse through these tomes reveals some of this year's hottest naming trends:

CELTIC NAMES

Boys: Tadhg, Deoradhain, Brachbhadhagan, Lymph

Girls: Kathleen, Kaitlyn, Katherkatelyn, Lymphoma

BIBLICAL NAMES

Boys: Aaron, Nebuchadnezzar, Burning Bush, God

Girls: Lot's Wife, Job's Wife, Noah's Wife and His Three Sons' Wives, An Unnamed Canaanite Woman

SURNAMES

Boys: Jackson, Travolta, Gyllenhaal, Yankovic

Girls: Palin, Winfrey, Kearns Goodwin, Klum

NAMES THAT ARE GOING TO SOUND DATED IN FIVE YEARS TOPS

Boys: Ryder, Landon, Barrett, anything rhyming with "laden"

Girls: Addison, Riley, Brianna, anything rhyming with "daily"

PLACE NAMES

Boys: Bryce, Zion, Yellowstone, Carlsbad Caverns

Girls: London, Paris, Brussels, Luxembourg City

PALINDROMES

Boys: Bob, Otto, Xanax, Jacobocaj

Girls: Ava, Elle, Hannah, Amanaplanacanalpanama

ROBOTS

Boys: T-800, R4-P17, HP-FRX-426999–435–87, HAL

Girls: FemiSapien, Actroid DER 2, 肺否捻鼻, Zellweger

VARIANT SPELLINGS

Boys: Mykul, Aanntthhoonnyy, E=van^2, David David Bo-Bavid Banana-Fana Fo-Favid Fee-Fi-Mo-Mavid David

Girls: M'Kenzie, Macncheese, Makinziti, *MACKENZIE* (italicized and all caps)

NAMES FOR THE TWO BEST KIDS IN THE WHOLE ENTIRE WORLD

Boys: N/A

Girls: Kate, Sara

CHAPTER 12

Labor and Delivery

Mom at Her Pushiest

And so, at long last, here you are. The hard work, the discipline, the endless days and nights pushing your body to its limits in nearly one-hundred-degree heat . . . they all come down to this. No one who witnesses what is about to transpire will ever forget your performance at this critical hour: your speed, your form, your positioning. Is it fair for your entire life up to this point to be judged solely on the outcome of this single moment? Perhaps not. But life is not always fair. Just ask one of the half billion dead sperm who'd have given their left centriole to be part of what's about to take place.

For those who go through it, birth is a deeply personal experience. To answer specific questions about the process seems cold and pointless. So for this climactic chapter, we will depart from our usual format and take a more intimate look by reprinting in its entirety the transcript of a panel discussion held at last month's convention of the American Academy of Neonatology in New York. The panel was entitled "The Out-of-the-Vagina

Monologues: Newborns Look Back on Their Births." The panelists were:

+ Annie Pruitt. One week old.
+ Harold Wilson. Five days old.
+ Clark Wu. Eight days old.
+ Dr. Eric Steinmetz, Chairman, Department of Obstetrics, Gynecology, and Reproductive Sciences, Yale School of Medicine. Four days old.

The moderator was Regis Philbin.

REGIS: First of all, thank you all for taking time out of your hectic schedules to join us here today.

HAROLD: Pleasure.

ANNIE: Great to be here, Reege.

ERIC: I'm just sorry you didn't bring Kelly. Rowrr! [*Laughs.*]

REGIS: Okay. Let's start at the beginning. When did you first realize labor was starting?

ANNIE: Around four in the afternoon last Monday. I was chilling out in my mom in the den listening to Oprah when all of a sudden I felt something that made the Braxton Hickses seem like back rubs.

ERIC: For me, it was at night. I was eight days overdue. I was pretty traumatized, having just gone through a near-birth experience. I was on the verge of getting induced when Daddy decided to try to, uh . . .

ANNIE: Induce you himself?

ERIC: Exactly. And it literally worked like a motherfucker. [*Laughs.*]

HAROLD: Mine started gradually. Mom's cervix had been effacing for some time, but I didn't think much of it. She's a very self-effacing person.

REGIS: What about you, Annie? Eric? Cervix effacement?

ANNIE: Oh, absolutely, Reege. It had gotten thin.

ERIC: *Real* thin.

ANNIE: Like one of those glass noodles they serve at Chinese restaurants.

HAROLD: And then a few days before this it just started . . . disappearing.

ERIC: Like someone was slowly opening up a sunroof.

ANNIE: It kept getting bigger. One centimeter . . .

HAROLD: Two centimeters . . .

ERIC: One inch. [*Glares at others.*] What is this, France?

REGIS: Clark, what can you tell us about your effacement?

CLARK: Not much, Regis. I was a scheduled C-section.

> [*Awkward silence.*]

REGIS: All right. So Annie, you're watching Oprah when the contractions start. How long between each one?

ANNIE: Twenty minutes. Two segments wth Dr. Oz and one commercial break. And they last about thirty-five seconds each.

REGIS: Eric, you're nodding your head.

ERIC: Same here. Thirty-five seconds. I know because I heard Daddy say "Mississippi" thirty-four times.

HAROLD: For me, the pauses *between* the contractions were even scarier.

ERIC: Oh yeah.

ANNIE: Definitely.

HAROLD: The suspense was . . . I mean, you *knew* what was coming.

ANNIE: And you *knew* it was coming quicker than last time.

ERIC: It was like the *Jaws* music.

REGIS: And what does being contracted feel like?

ERIC: Like Jaws. [*Laughs.*]

ANNIE: Like you're toothpaste in a tube.

ERIC: Like you're the meat layer of a lasagna squeezing itself vegetarian.

HAROLD: Like a snake is pooping you whole. Speaking of which . . . [*Poops.*]

ERIC: But the emotional pain was worse than the physical pain. Knowing you're no longer wanted, that you're being cast out.

REGIS: But there were valid reasons why you had to leave.

ERIC: I understand that. I'm just saying it was a nice place, and don't be surprised if I spend the rest of my life unconsciously trying to return there.

REGIS: Could you all tell you were going to the hospital? Here you go. [*Hands wipe to HAROLD.*]

HAROLD: Thanks. Yeah, I heard a lot of commotion, the car starting, Daddy schlepping a bag.

ERIC: Mom took a taxi. We got stuck in traffic. I was nervous. I had visions of having my cord bit off by a Korean cabdriver.

REGIS: That's what happened to Joey Bishop.

CLARK: I knew I was at the hospital because it was nine A.M. That's when the C-section was scheduled.

HAROLD: [*To CLARK.*] And that's when they started labor?

CLARK: No. There was no labor.

[*Gasps from panelists.*]

ERIC: What, you're too good for a little honest labor?

Common Male Labor Positions

Side lying

Squatting

Sitting

Hyperventilating

Kneeling

Drinking

Fleeing

Your Birthday:
Happy Draft Lottery to You!

The date on which you're born will become an annual celebration marked by cake, cards, and, as the years pass, morbid contemplation of approaching mortality. But some birthdays are happier than others.

January 1. Want your picture in the paper? Your cue is "Should old acquaintance be forgot."

February 14. If you're confident in your love life, go for it. Otherwise you're in for an annual double whammy of loneliness.

February 29. A terrible birthday. Average life expectancy of Leap Day babies: 18.7 years.

March 15. Really? Eleven other ides, and you choose this one?

April 1. Good luck getting anyone to take your birthday parties seriously.

April 20. Yes, it's "4/20," ha ha ha. It's also Hitler's birthday, jackass.

May 5 (Cinco de Mayo). *Ay ay ay!* Bring in your driver's license for a free Crunchwrap Supreme at Taco Bell! *Arriba arriba!*

REGIS: All right, settle down. What about you three? How long was labor?

ANNIE: Eight hours.

ERIC: Four hours.

HAROLD: Twenty-seven hours.

REGIS: Heyo!

HAROLD: Yeah, it was brutal. I'm not sure what Mom was thinking. If it were me, I'd have pushed me out as quickly as possible.

REGIS: You think she was deliberately stalling?

HAROLD: I didn't then. But now that I know her a little . . . I mean,

June 21. The start of summer ... and the end of any hope of a well-attended birthday party until September.

July 4. A perfect beginning to a career in politics.

July 14. *Un commencement parfait pour une carrière dans la politique.*

August 3. Completely unclaimed celebrity-wise. To make *Entertainment Tonight,* just outfame the bassist for the Stray Cats.

September 11. In a post-9/11 world, September 11 birthdays are *so* nineties.

October 31. Lots of candy every birthday! But next time, a little more effort with the costume.

November 21. The Scorpio/Sagittarius cusp day lends an unusual combination of ambition and intuitiveness to anybody who believes in bullshit like astrology.

December 25. Two reasons why this is the worst possible birthday: Your party can't compete with Christmas, and you can't compete with Christ.

she breast-feeds me for an hour and a half. She has closure issues, is all I'm saying.

REGIS: Do you all have any idea what's going on outside at this point?

HAROLD: When I felt the suction-cup thingie on my head I damn well did! Jeez. Nice that they extract you with the same technology that keeps shampoo on the side of the shower. [*Laughs.*]

CLARK: I had no idea, Reege. My folks always said they couldn't wait to go to "the hospital," but I thought that was just, like, the name of their second home or something.

Fecal Monitoring

Many mothers enter the delivery room with one overriding fear: that in the act of pushing out their baby, they will involuntarily poop. This concern is entirely founded. The potential embarrassment caused by inadvertent defecation is *exactly* what Mom should be focused on at this moment. If she begins to even suspect it has begun happening, she should break her pushing rhythm, take care of her business in the bathroom like a grown-up, and then start labor all over again. Only this time, with class.

ERIC: Yeah, I'll bet you did, C-boy.

CLARK: What's the matter? Jealous I took the express while you got stuck on the Vag Local?

ERIC: I don't know how things work "uptown," but where I come from those are crying words.

CLARK: You wanna cry? I'm right here!

ERIC: Then let's cry, motherfucker!

[*They cry.*]

REGIS: All right, all right, look, let's get some pacifiers up here and take a five-minute rocking break.

[*Later.*]

REGIS: We're back with our four newborns. Let's skip ahead to the big moment. Mom's fully dilated, the contractions have grown very intense, you've rotated your head 90 degrees to the occipito-anterior—

ANNIE: [*Impressed.*] Someone's done his research!

REGIS: I just read what's on the prompter. You're literally seconds away from birth. What's the first thing you feel that lets you know, "This incredible journey is about to begin"?

ANNIE: A draft.

HAROLD: Yeah, my scalp felt chilly.

ERIC: The first few seconds of life feel like an ice cream headache.

CLARK: With a C-section, like an ice cream headache all over your body.

ANNIE: I had no idea there was this whole reception committee waiting for me.

HAROLD: No, and I certainly had no idea they'd be invading my personal space like that.

ERIC: I was like, "Really? This is my first experience outside the womb? Some stranger touching me all over?"

CLARK: Last time I checked, that was called child molestation.

HAROLD: And he's got the gloves on.

CLARK: Like we're carrying a disease or something.

ANNIE: But what are you gonna do? He's got you in the palm of his hand.

ERIC: Oh, and then they ram some DustBuster up your nose and mouth.

HAROLD: Yeah. It's like, "No. That's my mucus! I'll get rid of it when I want to!"

ANNIE: And all this is happening while we're still chest-deep in the birth canal.

CLARK: Well, not me, but if anything, I felt even more intruded on.

ANNIE: So we let our feelings be known.

HAROLD: Loudly.

ERIC: We raised our voices in protest.

ANNIE: To me, at that moment, crying is about the healthiest thing you can do.

ERIC: Oh, and then snip! They cut the cord!

HAROLD: No warning!

CLARK: Just a complete disconnect.

ANNIE: I miss that cord!

[*Overlapping yelling.*]

REGIS: Okay, so a lot of anger at the medical community. But when you're finally being held by Mommy . . .

[*Instant silence. Group trance.*]

THE FIVE STAGES OF LABOR PAIN

Stage	Feels like . . .	Often described as . . .	Perceived duration
1	cervix overrun by lava	indescribable	1–2 hours
2	pelvis haunted by Ghost of Menses Past	unspeakable	2–3 days
3	commemorative plaque marked GEOGRAPHIC CENTER OF AGONY being riveted into tailbone	nonwordable	3–4 years
4	rectum = black hole sucking in all pain in galaxy	Weltzerstören*	4–5 millennia
5	vaginal 9/11	"FUUUUUUUUU-UUUUU—"	time transcended; there is only suffering

* German for "world-destroying."

ANNIE: Mommy.

HAROLD: Mommmmmmmy. Mommy Mommy Mommy. Boobs.

CLARK: Boobs Mommy. Mommy Boobs. Booby Moms. Moms Booby.

ERIC: Mommy boobooboobooboobooboo.

REGIS: Are you saying "boob"?

ERIC: No. "Boo." Mommy's bottle-feeding me. Bitch.

REGIS: Now that you've all had a few days to think about it, are you happy with how everything came out?

ERIC: You mean, the placenta? Yikes! [*Laughs.*] No, look, for all the problems and the trauma, it brought my parents and me together in a way that would otherwise have never been possible.

ANNIE: And the womb scene had gotten old and boring. So in a sense, birth was like a rebirth for me.

CLARK: I know what you mean. For me, as a Christian, being born felt like being born again, only first.

[*Awkward silence.*]

HAROLD: Coming out to my parents was one of the hardest things I've ever done. It took the better part of a year preparing for that one moment, and even when I thought I was ready, I spent most of the afternoon just getting myself to a place where I felt comfortable. But when I finally came out—once the truth of who I was emerged from those lips . . . it was like going from darkness into sunlight. All three of us hugged and cried for hours. I felt completely loved and accepted. Now my parents are totally supportive of my alternate lifestyle. [*Spits up.*]

REGIS: Well, thank you so much to our guests for joining us today. Any final bits of advice to our audience?

CLARK: Next time, come out Caesarean.

ANNIE: Live every moment like it's your first.

ERIC: There's always a light at the end of the tunnel. Sometimes you're just facing the wrong way.

HAROLD: [*Poops.*]

A Fetal Examination®

A POST-FETAL EXAMINATION

You're one minute old, and already there's a pop quiz. It's called the **Apgar test**, and it's what you've spent the last nine months crammed for. Passing it's a breeze if you know what they're looking for in all five sections:

Appearance (skin color). Pink = good; blue = bad. Good medicine . . . *or reverse sexism*?!

4. LACTATION : BREAST ::
   (A) urination : brain
   (B) sanitation : elbow
   (C) hypothesis : biologist
   (D) circulation : heart
   (E) ineptitude : Daddy

5. INFANT : SLEEP ::
   (A) thief: valuable
   (B) library: noise
   (C) tyrant : freedom
   (D) black hole : light
   (E) Joker : Batman

A major obstacle to Apgar success was removed with the elimination of the Analogies section in 2005.

Pulse. Double digits = dicey. Triple digits = good. Quadruple digits = hummingbird.

Grimace (reflex irritability). When stimulated by the doctor, react by coughing, pulling away, or ominously uttering, "You just made the list, buddy."

Activity (muscle tone). Shake ya ass, but watch ya self. Shake ya ass. Show them what you workin' with.

Respiration. Cry loudly—society doesn't expect you to suppress your emotions until you're *at least* two months old.

A perfect Apgar score is 10. The average score of this year's freshman class at Harvard was 9.932. Good luck!

In most cities, newborns are required to fill out their birth certificates within forty-eight hours of delivery or face a five-hundred-dollar fine. Opposite, a sample.

THE CITY OF NEW YORK
VITAL RECORDS CERTIFICATE
CERTIFICATE OF BIRTH

NEW YORK CITY   DEPARTMENT OF INFANT ACCOUNTABILITY

Birth No. 156—07—567234

FULL NAME OF CHILD
Last: **Rosenbaum**   First: **Ethan**   Middle: **Hussein**

DATE OF BIRTH
Year: **This**   Month: **This**   Day: **Yester**
time: **2:25:34 p.m. (crown of head)—2:26:32 p.m. (right big toe)**

PLACE OF BIRTH
Name of Facility: **Yoni's Midwifery and Womyn's Healthgarden**
Type of Facility: **Holistic birthing femmeporium**
Location in Facility: **The L Ward**

MOTHER'S NAME
Last: **Rosenbaum**   First: **Felicia**   Middle: **Middle (ha ha, Grandpa)**
Age: **At the moment, looks about sixty**
Race: **Swollen**
^ Occupation: **Biological clock**
Pre

FATHER'S NAME
Last: **Donor**   First: **A**   Middle: **Sperm**
Age: **25—30**
Race: **Caucasian/Jewish/AB+/Master's Degree or Better**
Occupation: **Nobel Prize—Winning Masturbator**

SECURITY INFORMATION
Number of family members traveling outside you: **1**
Have you or your carrying case been left unattended for any length of time? **No**
How long do you intend to stay in this country? **Through spring break Cancùn '26**
Primary purpose of your birth: **Spinning out my spool of destiny/giving Mom something to do**

VITAL RECORDS   DEPARTMENT OF INFANT ACCOUNTABILITY

I certify that the above stated information is true and correct to the best of my knowledge.

Signed: **Felicia M. Rosenbaum**, Mother/Witness

Above is your Certificate of Birth Registration. Under §3.21 of the New York City Health Code, this transcript may not be reproduced. Which is ironic.

ANY ALTERATION OR MECONIUM VOIDS THIS CERTIFICATE

CHAPTER 13

Months 10–1,000

A Time of Transition

O f the four hundred trimesters that make up the average human being's life, the first three are without question the most accomplished. However, the period that follows is marked by its own set of milestones, among them **childhood**, **adolescence**, **young adulthood**, **career**, **marriage**, **divorce**, **retirement**, and **death**. Of this postnatal–prefatal period, little can be said here that has not been explored more fully in a host of other works by such qualified medical professionals as Seuss, Phil, and Dre.

Our stated mission—to answer the questions and allay the fears of babies-to-be—has been fulfilled. If you have made it this far (and you haven't skipped ahead), congratulations. You are now a full-fledged *ex utero* human being, complete with a belly button, a Social Security number, and, assuming you would like to go home at any point in the near future, a rear-facing car seat.

We have focused on fetalcy from the logical point of view, that of you, the former fetus. But as this book and this chapter in your

Fig. 54. *Weeks 1,000–2,000 are frequently marked by a sharp increase in filing.*

life draw to a close, it is worth noting the two other people who have also been keenly following your progress.* No, you might not have seen much of them on your journey, and yes, in their sudden eagerness to bask in your success they may come across like the worst kind of talent agents. But in some indirect way, they, too, can claim a small measure of pride in your existence; and as you spend the next few months pursuing your hectic schedule of sleeping, crying, defecating, and other charitable work, it would behoove you to take a few moments to remember the two *big* people who made it all possible. Go ahead and give them a shout-out. Seriously, shout out. You'd be doing it anyway.

For Mommy and Daddy's work is just beginning. To them, the past nine months are but a prologue to the many years of parenting to come, when joy, sorrow, pride, guilt, contentment, frustration, uncertainty, and triumph will intermix like the ingredients of a V8 (Fig. 55). It won't always be easy for Mom and Dad to get that V8 down. Sometimes it will make them logy. Sometimes it will turn out to be the Spicy Hot V8. Or that awful new one, with fruit. Sometimes, they'll feel like pouring those V8s into a series of ever stiffer Bloody Marys that undermine the very foundation of your family. But at the end of the day they will always drink their V8, because deep down they

Fig. 55. *Parenthood tastes like Spaghetti-Os.*

* Hint: They are married, heterosexual, and acting in accordance with God's will.

know: Nothing makes them feel better, or more alive, than consuming 100 percent of their daily supply . . . of you.

Which brings us to one final irony.

ONE FINAL IRONY

"Which is what?"

This:

Right now, as you lie in your little bed, puffy-eyed, ink-footed, your pelvis-molded head bulging like western Africa, you may be thinking, "I wouldn't wish my last nine months on my worst enemy." Yet time heals all wounds, even C-scars; and many mitoses from now, you will most likely find yourself with an overwhelming urge to inflict this very same ordeal of fetushood on someone—and not just anyone, *but your own unborn child.* The tables will turn. The bab-ee will become the bab-er. And when that happens, you will discover that your experience of that child's life in the womb, though vicarious, will feel a million times more vivid and palpable and *alive* to you than anything you may have felt when you were actually living it. It doesn't make sense. It may even seem delusional. But it will happen, and it will give you a sense of where your parents are coming from, which is only fair, since they're where *you're* coming from.

Until that day, dear reader, get some sleep, drink plenty of boob, and poop like hell. Let us not leave with "good-bye." Rather, with mutual affection and delight, and in confidence that we will see each other once more, let us bid each other a fond . . ."peek-a-bieu."

ACKNOWLEDGMENTS

Thanks to Jon Stewart for his personal and professional example; Heidi Murkoff et al. for creating the template; David Miner, Nancy Rose, and Daniel Greenberg for their support and guidance; Spiegel & Grau for having faith; Chris Jackson for his calm exuberance and lapidary editing scalpel; and Mike Loew for breathing life into language with his extraordinary vision.

Above all, thanks to Mom, Dad, and Ali for a wonderful childhood, Kate and Sara for a wonderful parenthood, and Deb for a wonderful every-minute-of-every-day-of-my-lifehood.

DAVID JAVERBAUM has won nine Emmys and two Peabody Awards for his work as writer, head writer, and executive producer of *The Daily Show with Jon Stewart*. He was one of three principal authors of that show's 2004 bestseller, *America: The Book*. His work as a lyricist includes collaborating with composer Adam Schlesinger on the score for the Tony-nominated Broadway musical *Cry-Baby* and Stephen Colbert's television special *A Colbert Christmas: The Greatest Gift of All*. He lives in Manhattan with his wife, Debra, and their daughters, Kate and Sara.

PHOTO CREDITS